A MYSTERY QUILT ALONG

BY EBONY LOVE

2015 ENGLISH MANOR MYSTERY QUILT ALONG

Copyright © 2015 by Ebony Love.

All rights reserved.

The fabric images can only be used for the promotion and sale of the Andover Fabrics Downton Abbey Collection. Downton™ and Downton Abbey®© 2013-2104 Carnival Film & Television Limited. All rights reserved.

Photograph on page 20 by Weimar Meneses, provided under Creative Commons License. View the license at https://creativecommons.org/licenses/by/2.0/

AccuQuilt®, AccuQuilt Studio™, AccuQuilt GO!®, Studio™, Two Tone™ and GO!® are trademarks of AccuQuilt. Sizzix®, Sizzix BigShot™, fabi™, and BigShot Pro™ are trademarks of Ellison. EDeN™ System and Quilt Your Own Story™ are trademarks of LoveBug Studios. Use of any trademarks in this book does not imply affiliation or endorsement of the contents by their respective owners.

The book author retains sole copyright to her contributions to this book. No part of this book may be reproduced, stored in a retrieval system, or transmitted in any form, or by any means—electronic, mechanical, photocopying, recording, or otherwise—without prior written permission of the copyright holder, except as permitted under the 1976 United States Copyright Act.

We have done everything possible to ensure the accuracy of the information presented in this book, but no warranty or guarantee is provided for results achieved after implementing advice or techniques presented in this book. It is your responsibility to follow the recommendations of the original equipment manufacturer in order to preserve your rights and remedies under their warranty provisions. Neither the author nor people and entities associated with the publication of this book have any liability for loss or damage caused directly or indirectly by the information contained herein.

Printed in the United States of America

PUBLISHER: LoveBug Studios
DESIGNER: Brian Boehm, iDesign Graphics
TECHNICAL EDITOR: Linda Smoker
EDITOR: Anne K. DeRuiter

LoveBug Studios
1862 E. Belvidere Road. PMB 388
Grayslake, IL 60030

p: 877-577-8458

cust-service@lovebugstudios.com

lovebugstudios.com

ISBN: 978-1-938889-09-7 (PRINT)

ISBN: 978-1-938889-10-3 (DIGITAL)

TABLE of CONTENTS

Introduction 5
Preparing for your Adventure 6
Common Terminology 6
Fabric Preparation 6
Cutting Tips 9
Piecing Tips 10
Press, Clip and Swirl 11
Using Specialty Rulers 13

WEEK 1 — 15
INHERITANCE
The Mystery Begins

WEEK 2 — 21
ARISTOCRACY
Trip to Southhampton

WEEK 3 — 37
CONFIDANTE
Arriving at the Abbey

WEEK 4 — 49
ATTENDANT
A Gift from a Stranger

WEEK 5 — 59
CULINARIAN
Never Miss a Good Pudding

WEEK 6 — 71
COMPANION
Mimosas for Everyone

WEEK 7 — 83
FINALE
The Business of Life

WEEK 8 — 103
EGYPTOLOGY
The Egyptian Connection

Quilter's Gallery 111
EDeN System Chart 122

Special Thanks

So many people contributed to the success of the English Manor Mystery Quilt Along, and ultimately to the success of this special publication. I would like to extend a thank you to our Quilt Along sponsors, friends, supporters, independent quilt shops, staff and participants for making this such a fun and awesome experience.

- All About Quilts, Manhattan, KS
- Andover Fabrics
- Bayside Quilting, Olympia, WA
- Beaver Creek Mercantile, Caroline, AB   CANADA
- Blocks to Die For Staff
- Buttons and Bolts Fabric & Quilting Supply Inc., Salem, WI
- Charlotte's Cottage Quilt Shop, Walkersville, MD
- Claus ' En Paus Quilt Shop, Columbus, NE
- Creative Klutter, Irma, AB   CANADA
- Expressions in Threads, LeClaire, IA
- Fabrics Etcetera, Webster, TX
- Fat Quarter Shop, Manchaca, TX
- Four Pines Quilting, Claremont, NH
- From Past to Present, St. Clairsville, OH
- Happiness is Quilting, McKinney, TX
- Huntsville Sew & Vac, Huntsville, AL
- Little Quilts, Marietta, GA
- Madsen's Crafts, Idaho Falls, ID
- Mariner's Compass Quilt Shop, Bath, ME
- My Sewing Room, Calgary, AB   CANADA
- Nancy's Calico Patch, Newport News, VA
- Nuts for Bolts Etc., Red Deer, AB   CANADA
- Patchwork Garden, E. Amherst, NY
- Patchwork Plus, Dayton, VA
- Patchwork Plus, Marcellus, NY
- Peaceful Patch Quilt Shoppe, Blackfalds, AB   CANADA
- Pine Needles Quilt & Sew, Rochester, MN
- Prairie Flower Quilt Co., Leoti, KS
- Quilted Owl, Jefferson, LA
- Quilter's Quest, Woodridge, IL
- Quilters by the Square, Goderich, ON   CANADA
- Sew 'n Save Of Racine, Racine, WI
- Shoreline Handwerks, Manteo, NC
- Sizzix
- Stitch in the Ditch, Kelowna, BC   CANADA
- The Pin Cushion, Mitchell, SD
- The Quilt Corner, Baton Rouge, LA
- The Quilt Crossing, Boise, ID
- The Quilting Needle, Glenshaw, PA
- Winston's Sewing Center, St. Charles, MO

Introduction

I know you're super excited to get started, but before you dive right in, you should get familiar with how a *"Quilt Your Own Story™"* pattern works. If you remember how those chooseable path books worked when you were a kid, or when your own kids were reading, this concept is very similar.

In each chapter of this book, you'll be presented with a little story and offered the option to choose between sets of blocks. Depending on the path you choose, you'll be given instructions on how to cut and assemble each block set. It's important that you start from the beginning, and make your choices in the order in which they are presented.

Once you make your choice, you'll be directed to the page where your instructions begin. When your instructions for that set of blocks end, you'll be given the next page number to begin the next choice. By the end of the book, you'll have populated your "English Manor" with a fun set of characters, and the quilt will be uniquely your own!

There is no "right" or "wrong" way to choose blocks. All of them will work together to make a beautiful quilt. If you don't want the pressure of all the choices, go with the "Medley" path starting with the second block set for a sampler of all the blocks.

There are over 5,000 possible combinations for selecting blocks, so we hope you'll understand our not providing assembly directions for all possible scenarios. If you need some inspiration for assembling and arranging your own quilt, the Gallery near the back of the book provides some lovely examples of how other quilters built their English Manor quilts based on their own choices. When you finish your own quilt, we hope you'll share your photo with us too.

The preparation section reviews some tips and techniques to aid your cutting and piecing and will be helpful to you throughout your adventure. If you need more assistance, please create an account on our website so you can ask questions in our Forum for English Manor. Lots of quilters are still working on their quilts, so don't be shy!

Ebony Love

PREPARING FOR YOUR ADVENTURE

Before we begin the mystery quilt along, let's review some tips and techniques to aid your cutting and piecing. Whether you're a new quilter or an expert, it's a good idea to review the information in this section so you understand the terms we mention throughout the adventure.

Common Terminology

Quilters have a language all their own, and after a while, we start peppering our sentences with acronyms and all sorts of weird terms that may be unfamiliar to newer quilters. Here are some common terms and abbreviations you will see throughout this pattern.

HST—Half square triangle. This is a triangle that is made by cutting a square in half across one diagonal. You can recognize HSTs in a pattern because the squares they are cut from will usually end in ⅜" or ⅞".

QST—Quarter square triangle. This triangle is made by cutting a square in half across both diagonals. You can recognize QSTs in a pattern because the squares they are cut from will usually end in ¼" or ¾".

[ABC-x]—EDeN Numbers. Any abbreviations you see in brackets are instructions for die cutting. EDeN stands for Equivalent Die Notation, and it's a way to identify the correct dies for cutting the same sized units. If you are rotary cutting, just ignore any instructions in brackets. If you are die cutting, you should look up the EDeN Number in the reference chart to know what dies to use. Cut your strips based on your die layout.

Fabric Preparation

Whether you are using the Andover Fabrics line of Downton Abbey prints, or striking out with your own selections, it's important that you learn a little bit about your fabric and prepare it properly before you start. This section covers important tips to help you prepare your fabric in the best possible way to ensure success with your quilt.

Quilt by Number

To make it easy for you to follow a pattern designed for multiple color ways, we have numbered each fabric from 1 to 10. Each fabric keeps the same number throughout the entire quilt. In the cutting instructions, you will see a chart that shows the color number, plus a swatch from each color way. In the piecing instructions, you will only see the color number referenced.

For example, an instruction that refers to a "1-5-6 unit" means that unit uses fabrics 1, 5, and 6. The illustrations are all based on the Team Carson color way, but every block pattern shows you a finished block in each colorway so you can follow along.

If you are using your own fabric, we suggest creating your own color chart, numbering your fabrics 1-10, and using those fabrics in the same position throughout the quilt.

Yardage Assumptions

This quilt is defined by the choices you make as you move from block to block. As a result, the yardage calculations had to take into consideration the maximum amount of fabric that any particular block would use; the yardage was based on that, and rounded to the nearest ¼ yard.

After a block is made, any fabric which was cut from the yardage for that block may be completely used up, so the next block starts with a fresh cut. This is true whether you are using yardage cut from the bolt or fabric from a weekly block kit.

At the end, everyone will have fabric left over, and it may seem like a ridiculous amount in some cases. This is simply the tradeoff to have more freedom to choose the direction of your quilt without worrying about running out of fabric.

Initial cuts from fabric are made from strips cut selvage to selvage, also known as width of fabric (WOF). The directions assume the usable WOF is 40", even though your fabric may be wider. This measurement does not include the selvage, so make sure you remove the selvage before you start cutting units from your strips. The selvage is tightly woven, sometimes has large holes, and isn't always printed to the edge. This makes it hard to stitch through and can create inaccuracy when piecing.

For those who wish to save selvages for other projects and want longer pieces, you may safely remove the selvages in advance, but be sure to leave at least 40" of fabric behind, and keep your fabric folded selvage to selvage as you work so you don't confuse your fabric grain.

To Prewash or Not to Prewash?

Prewashing is a personal choice that is influenced by a number of factors, but whatever you decide, be consistent. If you're thinking about washing the red fabric because you think red tends to bleed more, then you should get ready to wash all of your fabrics. Cotton fabric tends to shrink in the 3-5% range, which amounts to a ½" loss per quarter yard of fabric. What you don't want to do is use fabric that's already shrunk next to a fabric that has more shrinking to do. You may not like the end result.

None of the fabrics for the sample quilts were prewashed, but a color catcher was added during the quilts' first washing in case any fabric bled.

If you have allergies, respiratory problems, or skin conditions that are aggravated by chemical residue, your health is best served by prewashing.

STRAIGHTENING YARDAGE

Don't let that crisp bolt-fold fool you! Fabric is rarely folded perfectly on-grain when it is rolled onto the bolt. If you're pre-washing, you have to iron the fabric anyway, but if you aren't, you should press out the bolt-fold and straighten your fabric. Here's how.

Hold the fabric up by the selvage edges, with your arms away from your body so you can see the fabric. Don't worry about straightening the entire length of fabric, just the part you can comfortably hold. When you do this, you may notice the fabric has a slight twist. That's what we need to eliminate.

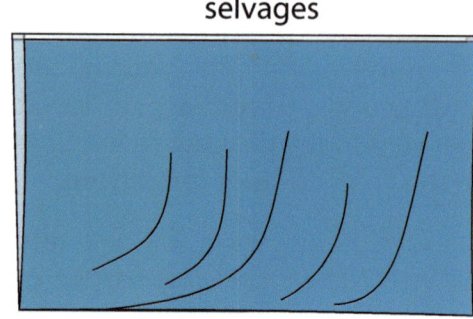
selvages

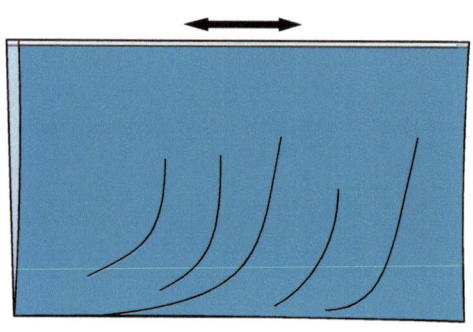

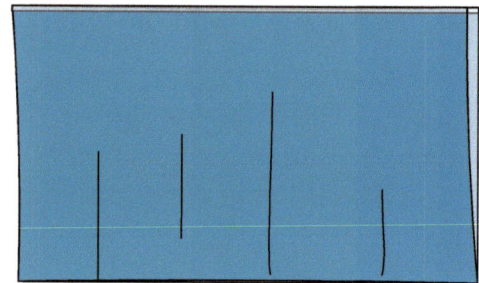

Keeping the selvage edges aligned as straight as possible, slide or shift one selvage to the left or right until the twist disappears.

After the twist disappears, carefully lay your fabric onto a cutting surface. Align an inch mark of a long, wide ruler along the bottom fold, and cut off the uneven raw edges. You now have a straight edge for cutting strips.

After making a few cuts, consider straightening your yardage again, especially if you weren't able to straighten the entire length of yardage the first time.

WORKING WITH DIRECTIONAL PRINTS

A directional print is any print that looks different based on the direction it is cut. Stripes, for example, can run vertically or horizontally depending on how you cut them and piece them into a block, and this can make a difference in the look of your finished block.

If it would bother you to have text reading sideways, or knit patterns upside down, or herringbones facing opposite directions, you may need to take a little more time planning your fabric placement before you begin piecing your blocks. If you are determined to have all your fabric oriented in one direction throughout the quilt, you may need to cut more pieces than we specify in the patterns in order to select the pieces that are oriented correctly.

What we try to do throughout the patterns is orient the directional fabrics in the most visually-pleasing way within the blocks. Anything more is up to you and your level of obsession with linearity.

Cutting Tips

Whether you are rotary cutting or die cutting, it's important to remember: safety first!

IF YOU ARE ROTARY CUTTING

- Use a new blade. When was the last time you changed the blade on your rotary cutter? If you have to press down hard in order to make a cut, it's time. Using dull blades is dangerous, and causes deep grooves in your cutting mats that are less likely to heal.

- Always cut away from yourself. This gives you more control over the cutter and is safer too.

- Hold the ruler firmly. Don't put your hand flat on the ruler; instead, tent your fingers and press down on the ruler as you make the cut. Make sure you keep your fingers away from the edge.

- Don't cross your arms. You should cut on the same side of your body as you hold the rotary cutter.

- Close the cutter EVERY TIME you put it down. It may feel like a waste of time, but it's easy to slice your hand open or lose a toe from a dropped or open cutter.

- Wear shoes. We hate sewing with shoes on, don't we? But in the event you do forget to close your cutter, or drop the scissors, you can keep all your toes.

IF YOU ARE DIE CUTTING

- Outline your dies. Do you know where the blades are? They are embedded in the foam in narrow slits that you can barely see. Outlining your shapes shows you where it's safe to put your fingers.

- Use both hands. It's tempting to just pick up a die with one hand, but what if you misjudge the weight, or don't get a firm grip?

- If you drop a die, let it fall and get out of the way. Resist the urge to grab at a falling die. You might grab it in the wrong place and get a serious cut.

- Don't overload the dies. Each die has a maximum number of layers that can be cut. GO® dies max out at 6; Sizzix® dies max out at 8; and Studio™ dies max out at 10 layers.

- Always use the mats that go with your machine. Cutting without a mat can damage your rollers, and cutting with the wrong mats can damage your die.

Piecing Tips

Quilting seams leave very little room for error — when you're working with ¼", every little bit counts, and even small errors add up over time.

Use the Right Needle and Thread

For piecing, we always recommend 75/11 or 80/12 quilting or topstitch needles. These needles are finer and have sharper points than the universal needles that are commonly used. The holes they create are smaller, meaning you'll pierce your fabric in the right place and increase the accuracy of your stitch.

To go with those needles, choose a 60- or 50-weight, 100% cotton thread. Either of these thread weights is a much finer thread than an all-purpose blend, leading to a narrower and more accurate seam. Cotton has a very high heat tolerance, which can withstand the pressing that we subject our blocks to. Threads with polyester content can melt at high temperatures, making it unsuitable for piecing (though using it for quilting is perfectly fine.)

Check Your Seam Allowance

Not every ¼" is created equal. Do you know whether you are stitching an accurate ¼" seam? In fact, we actually prefer stitching a scant ¼" (which is just one thread-width shy of ¼"). The scant seam allowance accommodates the tiny bit of width that you use from pressing a fabric over the seam allowance.

Reduce Your Stitch Length

Most machines come out of the box set to a 2.5mm stitch length. This stitch length is perfect for garment construction and home décor, but is too long for piecing. When using a 2.5mm stitch length, many quilters find it necessary to backstitch or lock stitches at the beginning of a seam so their units don't unravel, which creates unnecessary bulk and makes it difficult to orient seams. Instead, reduce your stitch length to 1.5 – 2.0mm, and eliminate the back stitch entirely.

Chain Piece for Efficiency

You can piece two blocks at a time, or even work on two projects at a time, so that you never have to cut threads. Chain piecing simply means that when you finish stitching one unit, you insert the next one right behind it and keep sewing. This method conserves thread, and makes your work more efficient. If you need to remove a set of units to press it or continue assembly, stitch onto a scrap (or onto another unit from a different section) until you are able to remove the set of units from the machine.

If you aren't chain piecing yet, try it! It will change the way you quilt forever.

Move Your Iron

It's tempting to have an iron set up right next to you at sewing height, so you never have to get up to press. Add in a rolling chair, and walking becomes nearly obsolete! However, getting up to press your units is an opportunity for you to take a break from being in one position, helps with circulation, and reduces stiffness. Take breaks to stretch too; it is fun to piece for long stretches at a time, but it's really hard on the body.

Press, Clip and Swirl

We use what we consider to be a unique approach to pressing units and blocks, which we will detail here. Our goal is to obtain flat, square blocks, and we will use every method we can to achieve this. We don't always press open, or always press to the dark; we press the direction we need to so the block is flat and square.

This may be unfamiliar territory for you, so when possible we give guidance on pressing seams during the block construction.

What it Means to Press

In quilting, we do not iron: we press.

Pressing fabric involves setting the iron down onto the fabric, and picking it up to move it to the next location, instead of sliding it from one place to another as we would do when ironing. Ironing stretches fabric, and the last thing you want to do is stretch your units out of shape.

After stitching each seam, press with the iron before opening it to set the seam. This settles your stitches into the fabric. Once your seam is set, open and press as directed.

We recommend an iron set to the highest setting for cotton fabrics, without steam. Introducing moisture during the piecing process can cause accuracy issues, especially if you haven't pre-washed. If you wish to starch your fabrics, do so at the beginning of the project, before you start cutting.

What it Means to Clip

Sometimes, we will have a unit with a seam pressed in one direction, but to attach it to a subsequent unit, we may need to twist the seam allowance. To prevent this twist from distorting the block, we use a pair of small, sharp scissors to clip into the seam and release the twist in the fabric.

When clipping, be careful not to clip your stitches or beyond them so you don't create a hole in your quilt.

We also recommend that you reduce your stitch length (between 1.5 – 2.0mm) so that your seams are stronger and able to withstand a clipped seam.

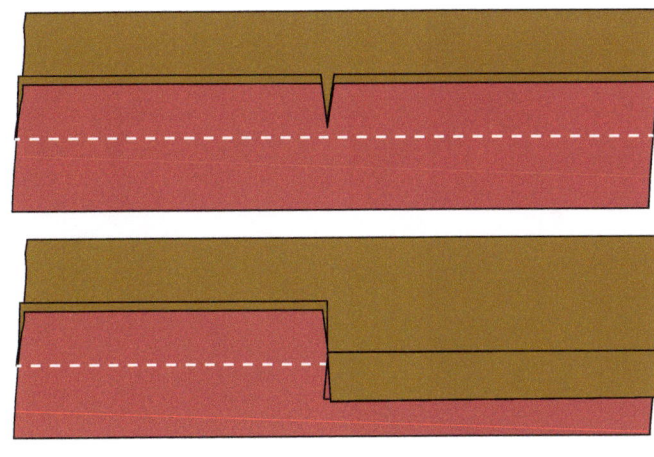

What it Means to Swirl

When multiple fabrics come together at an intersection, the best way to distribute bulk is to swirl the seams. This is a really common technique for four- and nine-patches, but you'd be surprised at how you can apply this technique to just about any block with intersections.

Swirling a seam properly requires planning ahead a bit when pressing seams, but if a seam isn't facing the right direction, you can always clip it to do the swirl.

To swirl a seam, work your way around the unit, pressing seams in a clockwise (or counterclockwise) direction. At the center, use your fingers to open up the seams so they also are pressed in the same direction.

You may need to use a seam ripper to remove 1-2 stitches at the center to allow it to open flat. Press the center from the back, then turn your block over and press it again from the front.

Using Specialty Rulers

There are so many ways to use tools, rulers, templates, and techniques to achieve accurate shapes for quilting. For this particular quilt, you may decide to use other methods, but we don't want you to be confused by the options. The pattern is written assuming that you will either use regular rotary or die cutting to make the quilt, but if you choose to use a specialty ruler or other technique, you can substitute the cutting instructions below.

Finished Size	Regular Ol' Rotary FOLLOW THE PATTERN	A Little Nervous About Accuracy (cut size)	Easy Angle or Half-Square Ruler (cut size)	Quarter Square or Companion Angle Ruler (cut size)	Die Cutting USE THE EDeN CHART
2" HST	Cut strips 2⅞"	Cut strips 3"; Square up to 2½" after sewing diagonal seam	Cut strips 2½"; black triangle is OFF strip; dog-ear corners	N/A	HST-2
3" HST	Cut strips 3⅞"	Cut strips 4"; Square up to 3½" after sewing diagonal seam	Cut strips 3½"; black triangle is OFF strip; dog-ear corners	N/A	HST-3
4" HST	Cut strips 4⅞"	Cut strips 5"; Square up to 4½" after sewing diagonal seam	Cut strips 4½"; black triangle is OFF strip; dog-ear corners	N/A	HST-4
5" HST	Cut strips 5⅞"	Cut strips 6"; Square up to 5½" after sewing diagonal seam	Cut strips 5½"; black triangle is OFF strip; dog-ear corners	N/A	HST-5
4" QST	Cut strips 5¼"	Cut strips 5½"; Square up to 4½" after sewing both diagonal seams	N/A	Cut strips 2½"; colored triangle is OFF strip; dog-ear corners	QST-4
5" QST	Cut strips 6¼"	Cut strips 6½"; Square up to 5½" after sewing both diagonal seams	N/A	Cut strips 3"; colored triangle is OFF strip; dog-ear corners	QST-5
6" QST	Cut strips 7¼"	Cut strips 7½"; Square up to 6½" after sewing diagonal seam	N/A	Cut strips 3½"; colored triangle is OFF strip; dog-ear corners	QST-6

STOP

BEFORE YOU CONTINUE,
HAVE YOU:

1. Read and understood that this is a Quilt Your Own Story™ Pattern? It means you shouldn't skip around and you shouldn't make every block on every page. **Turn back to page 5 if you need help.**

2. Read the note about directional prints? **Turn to page 8 for more info.**

3. Decided whether you are rotary cutting or die cutting? **Read about Cutting Tips on page 9** so you understand how to read the pattern for rotary or die cutting.

4. Watched Downton Abbey at all? If not, think about it. You might get some of the jokes about the characters as you read through the story.

5. Relaxed so you can enjoy yourself?

Have fun!

To begin your adventure,
CONTINUE TO PAGE 15

Inheritance
Week One

The Mystery Begins...

You receive a curious letter in the mail, on official-looking letterhead, stating that you are heir to an estate in Southampton, Great Britain. You are asked to travel there and inspect the property, and enclosed with the letter is a plane ticket and prepaid American Express card for expenses.

It's hard to believe that such a letter could be real, especially in this day and age. You've seen enough Nigerian Prince emails to know what's what, and no one's going to fool you. However, the letter encourages you to call the British Consulate in your country to verify the information. Not trusting the phone number given in the letter, of course, you Google it to find the correct number. To your great surprise, the telephone numbers match!

You speak to the Consul General and he confirms that everything is legitimate, and congratulates you on your inheritance.

The plane ticket is dated for today. This afternoon, in fact! But you have a job, family, obligations. You have quilts to make! Cat videos to watch! Why on earth would you pick up everything and leave right now for the UK?

If you get on the plane, go to Manor House, page 17.

If you decide to stay home, go to Your House, page 20.

Manor House
GO TO PAGE **17**

Your House
GO TO PAGE **20**

Need More Help?

This project is available as an online class!

Get instant access to videos, full-color photo tutorials, and our exclusive website Forum for additional support.

We invite you to ask questions, post photos, and get help from other quilters. Why do this alone when you can join thousands of other quilters in this amazing experience?

English Manor
Mystery Quilt Along

http://eLBS.us/EM

Use coupon code **EMBOOK5** at checkout and save $5 on the class.

Manor House

MAKE 1

Finished Block Size: 20" x 20"
Unfinished Block Size: 20½" x 20½"

Cutting

Color #	Team Cora	Team Carson	Team Rose	Cutting
1	A-7598-R	A-7597-B	A-7614-EC	Cut a 5⅞" x WOF strip. From this, cut (2) 5⅞" squares. Cut along one diagonal for (4) HSTs. [HST-5]
2	A-7332-K1	A-7666-RK	A-7332-B1	Cut a 5⅞" x WOF strip. From this, cut (4) 5⅞" squares. Cut along one diagonal for (8) HSTs. [HST-5]
3	A-7330-ET	A-7332-R	A-7616-EG	Cut a 6¼" x WOF strip. From this, cut (1) 6¼" square. Cut along both diagonals for (4) QSTs. [QST-5]
4	A-7617-C	A-7617-N	A-7613-E	Cut a 5⅞" x WOF strip. From this, cut (2) 5⅞" squares. Cut along one diagonal for (4) HSTs. [HST-5]
6	A-7598-B	A-7598-B	A-7616-BG	Cut a 6¼" x WOF strip. From this, cut (2) 6¼" squares. Cut along both diagonals for (8) QSTs. [QST-5]
7	A-7665-B	A-7332-B1	A-7615-B	Cut a 6¼" x WOF strip. From this, cut (2) 6¼" squares. Cut along both diagonals for (8) QSTs. [QST-5]
8	A-7665-R	A-7666-BN	A-7616-BP	Cut a 5⅞" x WOF strip. From this, cut (2) 5⅞" squares. Cut along one diagonal for (4) HSTs. [HST-5]
9	A-7597-G	A-7602-K	A-7597-R	Cut a 6¼" x WOF strip. From this, cut (1) 6¼" square. Cut along both diagonals for (4) QSTs. [QST-5]

Assembly

1. Sew the short side of (1) Fabric 3 QST to the short side of (1) Fabric 9 QST as shown to make a 3-9 pieced triangle. Press seam open. Make 4.

2. Sew the long side of (1) pieced triangle to the long side of (1) Fabric 8 HST as shown to make a 3-9-8 square measuring 5½" x 5½". Press seam to the Fabric 8 HST. Make 4.

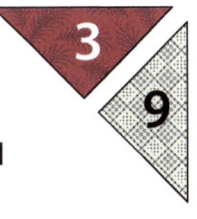 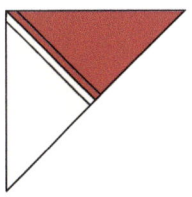 

3. Repeat steps 1 & 2 using (1) Fabric 6 QST, (1) Fabric 7 QST and (1) Fabric 4 HST as shown to make a 6-7-4 square measuring 5½" x 5½". Press seam to the Fabric 4 HST. Make 4.

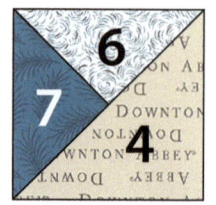

4. Repeat steps 1 & 2 using (1) Fabric 6 QST, (1) Fabric 7 QST and (1) Fabric 2 HST as shown to make a 6-7-2 square measuring 5½" x 5½". Press seam to the Fabric 2 HST. Make 4.

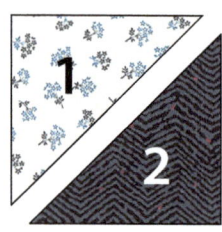  

5. Sew the long side of (1) Fabric 1 HST to the long side of (1) Fabric 2 HST as shown to make a 1-2 square measuring 5½" x 5½". Press seam to the Fabric 2 HST. Make 4.

6. Lay out the 16 squares in 4 rows of 4 squares each, noting the orientation and placement of each square.

7. Sew the squares together in each row. Join the rows to make a 20½" x 20½" Manor House block. Clip, swirl and press seams as necessary to achieve a flat seam.

Inheritance, Week 1 ❖ English Manor Mystery Quilt Along

Team Cora

Team Carson

Team Rose

TO CONTINUE YOUR ADVENTURE,
JUMP TO PAGE 21

Your House

So you decided to stay home and watch cat videos instead
of claiming a fabulous estate in Southampton?
I can't believe you're ending your adventure before
you really begin, but I understand the attraction of kitty hijinx.
They are nearly irresistible, aren't they?
Since you won't be joining us on the rest of the adventure,
we'll leave you to watch your precious cats.

Funny Cat Video: http://elbs.us/catvideo

The End. Meow!

It's not too late to start over,
GO BACK TO PAGE **15**

Aristocracy
Week Two

The Trip to Southampton...

You pack your bags and head to the airport as fast as you can. With your heart pumping, you breeze through security, and board the airliner just in time. You settle into your First-Class seat, accept a mimosa from the flight attendant, and daydream about the beautiful estate you're about to claim.

As the plane starts to taxi down the runway, you feel the familiar rumble of the wheels against the pavement and the plane picks up speed. All of a sudden, while you're sipping your mimosa, you start to feel a little woozy. Your vision starts to get grainy, and as you reach for the call button for help (fat chance during takeoff), you pass out.

When you wake up (minutes? hours?) later, you're dimly aware that something has changed. You still feel the rumble of pavement, but you're no longer in a plane. You're in a car. In a Ford Model T. You bolt upright in your seat. You're in Southampton for sure, but this is not 2015. It's 1924.

You call out to the driver to STOP! He turns around and you notice immediately that it's Branson. But that can't be right. Branson is not a chauffeur anymore. Everything is mixed up in your head. You open the door and stumble out of the car. Your foot catches on the curb and you bump into someone. You look up and see a familiar face. It's… it's…

If the person you bumped into is Countess Cora, go to Lady's Tiara, page 22.
If the person you bumped into is the Earl of Grantham, go to Earl's Pipe, page 26.
If you bump into them both, go to Aristocracy Medley, page 30.

Lady's Tiara
GO TO PAGE **22**

Earl's Pipe
GO TO PAGE **26**

Aristocracy Medley
GO TO PAGE **30**

Lady's Tiara
MAKE 4

Finished Block Size: 12" x 12"
Unfinished Block Size: 12½" x 12½"

Cutting

Color #	Team Cora	Team Carson	Team Rose	Cutting
2	A-7332-K1	A-7666-RK	A-7332-B1	Cut a 7¼" x WOF strip. From this, cut (4) 7¼" squares. Cut along both diagonals for (16) QSTs. [QST-6]
4	A-7617-C	A-7617-N	A-7613-E	Cut a 4⅞" x WOF strip. From this, cut (8) 4⅞" squares. Cut along one diagonal for (16) HSTs. [HST-4]
5	A-7332-R	A-7332-N	A-7615-E	Cut a 7¼" x WOF strip. From this, cut (2) 7¼" squares. Cut along both diagonals for (8) QSTs. [QST-6] From remaining strip length, cut (2) 2⅞" strips. From this, cut (8) 2⅞" squares. Cut along one diagonal for (16) HSTs. [HST-2]
8	A-7665-R	A-7666-BN	A-7616-BP	Cut a 7¼" x WOF strip. From this, cut (2) 7¼" squares. Cut along both diagonals for (8) QSTs. [QST-6] From remaining strip length, cut (2) 2⅞" strips. From this, cut (8) 2⅞" squares. Cut along one diagonal for (16) HSTs. [HST-2]
10	A-7598-N	A-7601-G	A-7598-N	Cut (3) 2⅞" x WOF strips. From this, cut (24) 2⅞" squares. Cut along one diagonal for (48) HSTs. [HST-2]

Assembly

1. Sew the long side of (1) Fabric 10 HST to the long side of (1) Fabric 5 HST as shown to make a 2½" x 2½" 10-5 HST. Press seam open. Make 16.

2. Sew (2) 10-5 HSTs together to make a 2½" x 4½" two-piece unit. Press seam open. Sew (1) Fabric 10 HST to the end of the two-piece unit as shown. Press seam open. Make 8.

  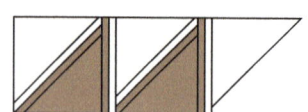 

3. Sew the short side of (1) Fabric 4 HST to the bottom of the unit to make pieced triangle #1. Press seam to Fabric 4 triangle. Make 8.

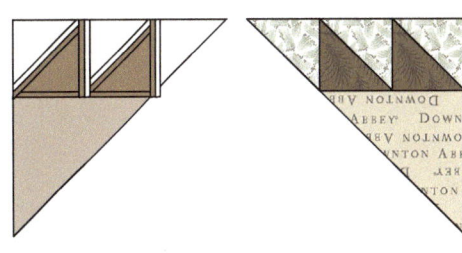

4. Sew the short side of (1) Fabric 8 QST to the short side of (1) Fabric 2 QST to make pieced triangle #2. Press seam open. Make 8.

5. Sew the long side of pieced triangle #1 to the long side of pieced triangle #2 to make a 6½" x 6½" Block A. Clip and press seam as necessary to achieve a flat seam. Make 8.

  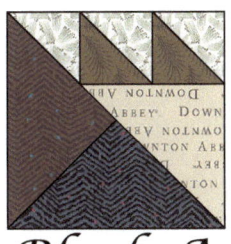

Block A

6. Sew the long side of (1) Fabric 10 HST to the long side of (1) Fabric 8 HST as shown to make a 2½" x 2½" 10-8 HST. Press seam open. Make 16.

7. Sew (2) 10-8 HSTs together to make a 2½" x 4½" two-piece unit. Press seam open. Sew (1) Fabric 10 HST to the end of the two-piece unit as shown. Press seam open. Make 8.

8. Sew the short side of (1) Fabric 4 HST to the bottom of the unit to make pieced triangle #1. Press seam to Fabric 4 triangle. Make 8.

 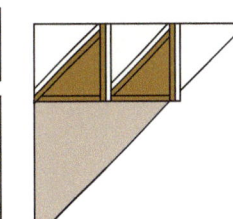 

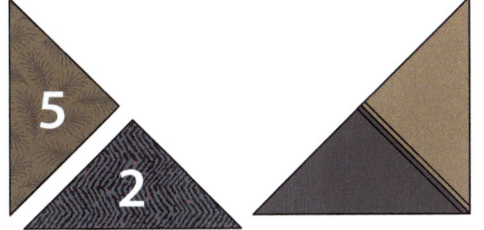 

9. Sew the short side of (1) Fabric 5 QST to the short side of (1) Fabric 2 QST to make pieced triangle #2. Press seam open. Make 8.

English Manor Mystery Quilt Along ❖ Aristocracy, Week 2

10. Sew the long side of pieced triangle #1 to the long side of pieced triangle #2 to make a 6½" x 6½" Block B. Clip and press seam as necessary to achieve a flat seam. Make 8.

  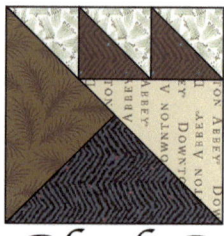

Block B

11. Lay out (2) A blocks, alternating with (2) B blocks in 2 rows of 2 blocks each, noting the orientation and placement of each block.

12. Sew the blocks together in each row. Join the rows to make a 12½" x 12½" Lady's Tiara block. Clip, swirl and press seams as necessary to achieve a flat seam. Make 4 blocks.

Block A   Block B

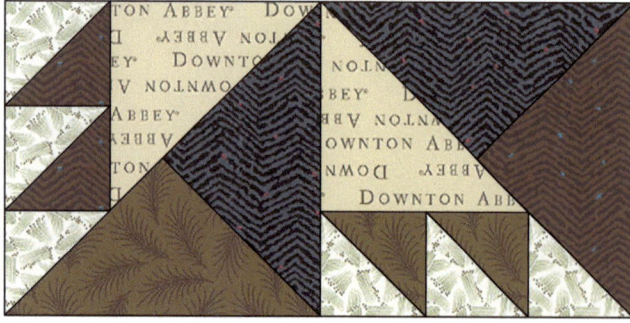

Block B   Block A

Team Cora

Lady's Tiara - Make 4

Team Carson

Team Rose

To continue your adventure,
JUMP TO PAGE 37

Earl's Pipe
MAKE 4

Finished Block Size: 12" x 12"
Unfinished Block Size: 12½" x 12½"

Cutting

Color #	Team Cora	Team Carson	Team Rose	Cutting
2	A-7332-K1	A-7666-RK	A-7332-B1	Cut (2) 2⅞" x WOF strips. From this, cut (20) 2⅞" squares. Cut along one diagonal for (40) HSTs. [HST-2]
4	A-7617-C	A-7617-N	A-7613-E	Cut a 7¼" x WOF strip. From this, cut (4) 7¼" squares. Cut along both diagonals for (16) QSTs. [QST-6]
5	A-7332-R	A-7332-N	A-7615-E	Cut a 4⅞" x WOF strip. From this, cut (4) 4⅞" squares. Cut along one diagonal for (8) HSTs. [HST-4]
8	A-7665-R	A-7666-BN	A-7616-BP	Cut a 7¼" x WOF strip. From this, cut (4) 7¼" squares. Cut along both diagonals for (16) QSTs. [QST-6]
10	A-7598-N	A-7601-G	A-7598-N	Cut an 11" x WOF strip. From this, cut an 11" x 21" rectangle and an 11" x 6" rectangle. From the 11" x 6" rectangle, cut (6) 2⅞" squares. Cut along one diagonal for (12) HSTs. [HST-2] From the 11" x 21" rectangle, cut (2) 2⅞" x 21" strips and (1) 4⅞" x 21" strip. From the 2⅞" strips, cut (14) 2⅞" squares. Cut along one diagonal for (28) additional Unit A HSTs, and a total of (40) HSTs. [HST-2] From the 4⅞" strips, cut (4) 4⅞" squares. Cut along one diagonal for (8) HSTs. [HST-4]

Assembly

1. Sew the long side of (1) Fabric 10 HST to the long side of (1) Fabric 2 HST as shown to make a 2½" x 2½" 10-2 HST. Press seam to the Fabric 2 triangle. Make 40.

2. Sew (2) 10-2 HSTs together as shown to make a 2½" x 4½" two-piece unit. Clip and press seams as necessary to achieve a flat seam. Make 8.

3. Sew (3) 10-2 HSTs together as shown to make a 2½" x 6½" three-piece unit. Clip and press seams as necessary to achieve a flat seam. Make 8.

4. Sew the long side of (1) Fabric 10 HST to the long side of (1) Fabric 5 HST as shown to make a 10-5 HST measuring 4½" x 4½". Press seam to the Fabric 5 triangle. Make 8.

5. Sew the two-piece unit to the left side of the HST (see illustration below). Clip and press seam as necessary to achieve a flat seam.

6. Sew the three-piece unit to the adjacent side of the HST as shown to make a 6½" x 6½" Block A. Clip and press seam as necessary to achieve a flat seam. Make 8.

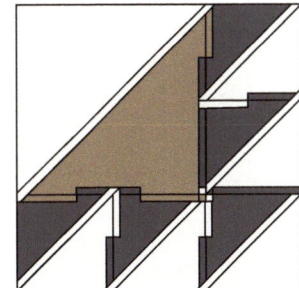

Block A

7. Sew the short side of (1) Fabric 8 QST to the short side of (1) Fabric 4 QST to make pieced triangle. Press to the Fabric 8 triangle. Make 16.

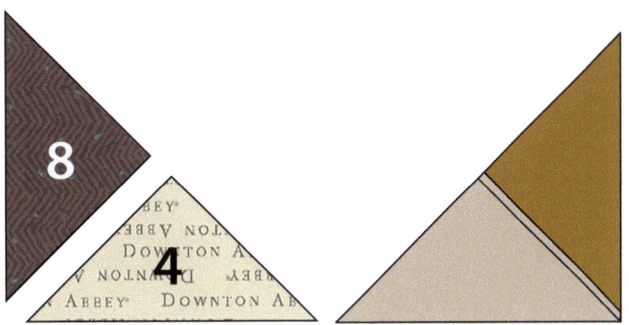

English Manor Mystery Quilt Along ❖ Aristocracy, Week 2

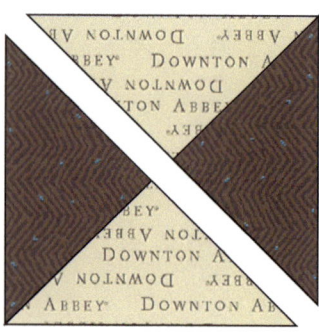  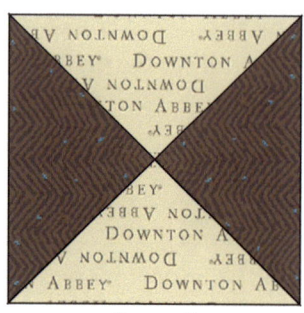

8. Sew the long sides of (2) pieced triangles to make a 6½" x 6½" Block B. Clip, swirl and press seams as necessary to achieve a flat seam. Make 8.

Block B

9. Lay out (2) A blocks, alternating with (2) B blocks in 2 rows of 2 blocks each, noting the orientation and placement of each block.

10. Sew the blocks together in each row. Join the rows to make a 12½" x 12½" Earl's Pipe block. Clip, swirl and press seams as necessary to achieve a flat seam. Make 4 blocks.

Team Cora

Earl's Pipe - Make 4

Team Carson

Team Rose

To continue your adventure,
JUMP TO PAGE 37

Aristocracy Medley

Lady's Tiara – MAKE 2 | Earl's Pipe – MAKE 2

Finished Block Sizes: 12" x 12"
Unfinished Block Sizes: 12½" x 12½"

Cutting

Color #	Team Cora	Team Carson	Team Rose	Cutting
2	 A-7332-K1	 A-7666-RK	 A-7332-B1	Cut a 7¼" x WOF strip. From this, cut (2) 7¼" squares. Cut along both diagonals for (8) QSTs. [QST-6] From remaining strip length, cut (2) 2⅞" strips. From this, cut (10) 2⅞" squares. Cut along one diagonal for (20) HSTs. [HST-2]
4	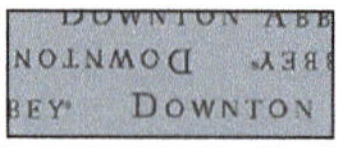 A-7617-C	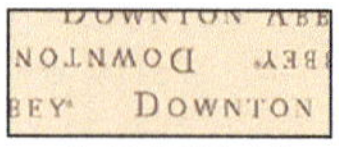 A-7617-N	 A-7613-E	Cut a 7¼" x WOF strip. From this, cut (2) 7¼" squares. Cut along both diagonals for (8) QSTs. [QST-6] From remaining strip length, cut (4) 4⅞" squares. Cut along one diagonal for (8) HSTs. [HST-4]
5	 A-7332-R	 A-7332-N	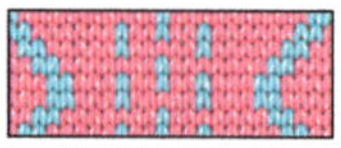 A-7615-E	Cut a 7¼" x WOF strip. From this, cut (1) 7¼" square. Cut along both diagonals for (4) QSTs. [QST-6] From remaining strip length, cut (1) 4⅞" x 10" rectangle. From this, cut (2) 4⅞" squares. Cut along one diagonal for (4) HSTs. [HST-4] From remaining strip length, cut (2) 2⅞" strips. From this, cut (4) 2⅞" squares. Cut along one diagonal for (8) HSTs. [HST-2]
8	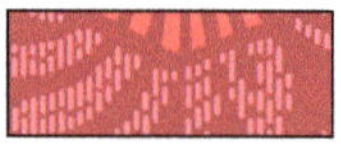 A-7665-R	 A-7666-BN	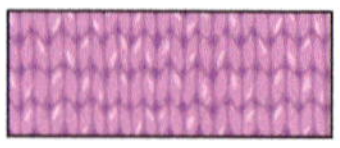 A-7616-BP	Cut a 7¼" x WOF strip. From this, cut (3) 7¼" squares. Cut along both diagonals for (12) QSTs. [QST-6] From remaining strip length, cut (2) 2⅞" x 6" rectangles. From this, cut (4) 2⅞" squares. Cut along one diagonal for (8) HSTs. [HST-2]
10	 A-7598-N	 A-7601-G	A-7598-N	Cut (1) 11" x WOF strip. From this, cut (2) 2⅞" x 27" strips and (1) 4⅞" x 27" strip. From the (2) 2⅞" strips, cut (18) 2⅞" squares. Cut along one diagonal for (36) HSTs. [HST-2] From the 4⅞" strip, cut (2) 4⅞" squares. Cut along one diagonal for (4) HSTs. [HST-4] From the remaining 4⅞" strip length, cut (4) 2⅞" squares. Cut along one diagonal for (8) more HSTs. You will have a total of (44) HSTs. [HST-2]

Lady's Tiara
[Make 2]

Assembly

1. Sew the long side of (1) Fabric 10 HST to the long side of (1) Fabric 5 HST as shown to make a 2½" x 2½" 10-5 HST. Press seam open. Make 8.

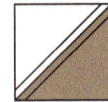

2. Sew (2) 10-5 HSTs together to make a 2½" x 4½" two-piece unit. Press seam open. Sew (1) Fabric 10 HST to the end of the two-piece unit as shown. Press seam open. Make 4.

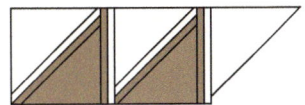

3. Sew the short side of (1) Fabric 4 HST to the bottom of the unit to make pieced triangle #1. Press seam to Fabric 4 triangle. Make 4.

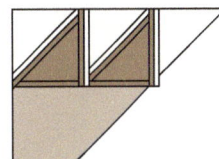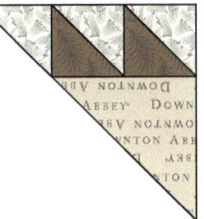

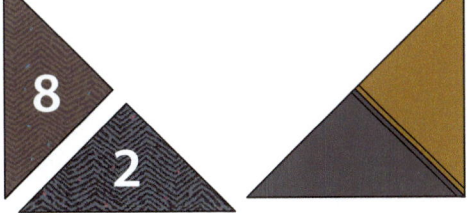

4. Sew the short side of (1) Fabric 8 QST to the short side of (1) Fabric 2 QST to make pieced triangle #2. Press seam open. Make 4.

5. Sew the long side of pieced triangle #1 to the long side of pieced triangle #2 to make a 6½" x 6½" Block A. Clip and press seam as necessary to achieve a flat seam. Make 4.

Block A

6. Sew the long side of (1) Fabric 10 HST to the long side of (1) Fabric 8 HST as shown to make a 2½" x 2½" 10-8 HST. Press seam open. Make 8.

7. Sew (2) 10-8 HSTs together to make a 2½" x 4½" two-piece unit. Press seam open. Sew (1) Fabric 10 HST to the end of the two-piece unit as shown. Press seam open. Make 4.

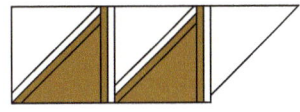

8. Sew the short side of (1) Fabric 4 HST to the bottom of the unit to make pieced triangle #1. Press seam to Fabric 4 triangle. Make 4.

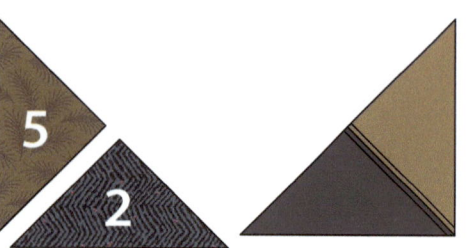

9. Sew the short side of (1) Fabric 5 QST to the short side of (1) Fabric 2 QST to make pieced triangle #2. Press seam open. Make 4.

10. Sew the long side of pieced triangle #1 to the long side of pieced triangle #2 to make a 6½" x 6½" Block B. Clip and press seam as necessary to achieve a flat seam. Make 4.

Block A *Block B*

Block B

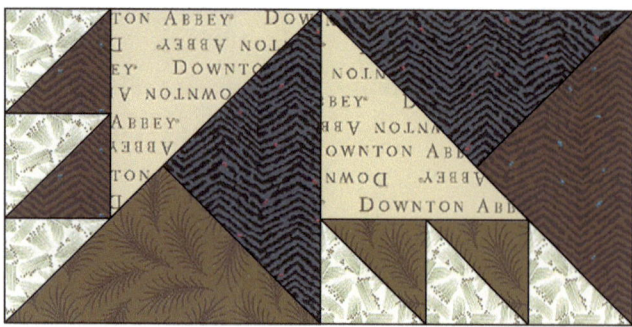

Block B *Block A*

11. Lay out (2) A blocks, alternating with (2) B blocks in 2 rows of 2 blocks each, noting the orientation and placement of each block.

12. Sew the blocks together in each row. Join the rows to make a 12½" x 12½" Lady's Tiara block. Clip, swirl and press seams as necessary to achieve a flat seam. Make 2 blocks.

Team Cora

Lady's Tiara - Make 2

Team Carson

Team Rose

CONTINUE TO NEXT PAGE ▶

English Manor Mystery Quilt Along ❖ Aristocracy, Week 2

Earl's Pipe
[MAKE 2]

Assembly

1. Sew the long side of (1) Fabric 10 HST to the long side of (1) Fabric 2 HST as shown to make a 2½" x 2½" 10-2 HST. Press seam to the Fabric 2 triangle. Make 20.

2. Sew (2) 10-2 HSTs together as shown to make a 2½" x 4½" two-piece unit. Clip and press seams as necessary to achieve a flat seam. Make 4.

3. Sew (3) 10-2 HSTs together as shown to make a 2½" x 6½" three-piece unit. Clip and press seams as necessary to achieve a flat seam. Make 4.

4. Sew the long side of (1) Fabric 10 HST to the long side of (1) Fabric 5 HST as shown to make a 10-5 HST measuring 4½" x 4½". Press seam to the Fabric 5 HST. Make 4.

5. Sew the two-piece unit to the left side of the HST (see illustration below). Clip and press seam as necessary to achieve a flat seam.

6. Sew the three-piece unit to the adjacent side of the HST as shown to make a 6½" x 6½" Block A. Clip and press seam as necessary to achieve a flat seam. Make 4.

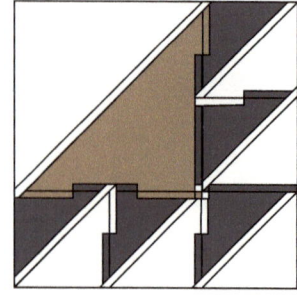

Block A

7. Sew the short side of (1) Fabric 8 QST to the short side of (1) Fabric 4 QST to make pieced triangle. Press to the Fabric 8 triangle. Make 8.

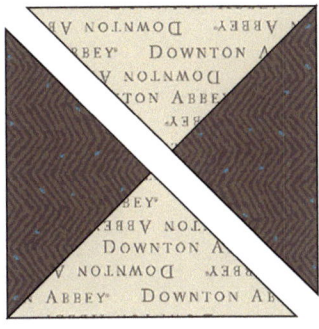  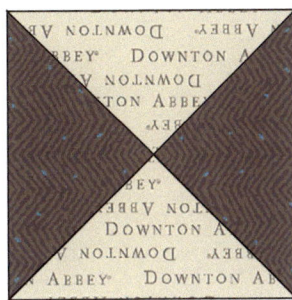

8. Sew the long side of (2) pieced triangles together to make a 6½" x 6½" Block B. Clip, swirl and press seams as necessary to achieve a flat seam. Make 4.

Block B

Block B   Block A

Block A   Block B

9. Lay out (2) A blocks, alternating with (2) B blocks in 2 rows of 2 blocks each, noting the orientation and placement of each block.

10. Sew the blocks together in each row. Join the rows to make a 12½" x 12½" Earl's Pipe block. Clip, swirl and press seams as necessary to achieve a flat seam. Make 2 blocks.

English Manor Mystery Quilt Along ❖ Aristocracy, Week 2

Team Cora

Earl's Pipe - Make 2

Team Carson

Team Rose

To continue your adventure,
READ THE NEXT PAGE ▶

Confidante
Week Three

Arriving at the Abbey...

Well it's not every day that you bump into someone who's practically royalty! You beg their pardon, exchange pleasantries, and before you know it, you've secured an invitation to dine at Downton Abbey that evening. Perhaps sensing your bewildering predicament, they ask you to come early so they can assist you in dressing appropriately for dinner. You stammer out an acceptance as they continue their stroll down the avenue.

As promised, you arrive on the doorstep of Downton Abbey and are greeted by Carson the butler, who shows you into the drawing room. One of the maids shows you upstairs to what is to be your dressing room. Miraculously, there's an outfit waiting for you. It's your favorite ensemble from the show, in your perfect size, and very appropriate for a 1920s dinner.

You half expected someone to be in the room helping you get dressed or finish your toilette, but after waiting several minutes, you decide to make a go of it yourself. After all, you've been dressing yourself since you were 5 years old, and there's no sense in having done what you can do yourself.

As you are admiring your handiwork and buttoning the last button, there's a knock at the door, and you hear a familiar voice. It's one of the lady's maids, and she has something important to tell you. You feel a little giddy at the idea of meeting with more familiar faces. You open the door, and standing in the corridor you find…

**If the person standing in the corridor is Anna Bates, go to Anna's Affection, page 38.
If the person standing in the corridor is Sarah O'Brien, go to Sarah's Daring, page 41.
If they are both standing in the corridor, go to Medley, page 44.**

Anna's Affection
GO TO PAGE **38**

Sarah's Daring
GO TO PAGE **41**

Confidante Medley
GO TO PAGE **44**

Anna's Affection

Make 8

Finished Block Size: 12" x 12"
Unfinished Block Size: 12½" x 12½"

Cutting

Color #	Team Cora	Team Carson	Team Rose	Cutting
1	A-7598-R	A-7597-B	A-7614-EC	Cut (4) 3⅞" x WOF strips. From this, cut (32) 3⅞" squares. Cut along one diagonal for (64) HSTs. [HST-3]
3	A-7330-ET	A-7332-R	A-7616-EG	Cut (2) 3⅞" x WOF strips. From this, cut (16) 3⅞" squares. Cut along one diagonal for (32) HSTs. [HST-3]
5	A-7332-R	A-7332-N	A-7615-E	Cut (2) 3⅞" x WOF strips. From this, cut (16) 3⅞" squares. Cut along one diagonal for (32) HSTs. [HST-3]
7	A-7665-B	A-7332-B1	A-7615-B	Cut (4) 3⅞" x WOF strips. From this, cut (32) 3⅞" squares. Cut along one diagonal for (64) HSTs. [HST-3]
9	A-7597-G	A-7602-K	A-7597-R	Cut (4) 3⅞" x WOF strips. From this, cut (32) 3⅞" squares. Cut along one diagonal for (64) HSTs. [HST-3]

Assembly

1. Sew the long side of (1) Fabric 7 HST to the long side of (1) Fabric 9 HST as shown to make a 3½" x 3½" 7-9 HST. Press seam to Fabric 7. Make 32.

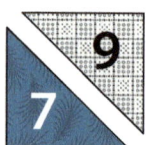 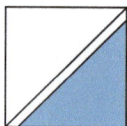 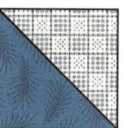

2. Sew the long side of (1) Fabric 7 HST to the long side of (1) Fabric 1 HST as shown to make a 3½" x 3½" 7-1 HST. Press seam to Fabric 7. Make 32.

 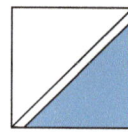 

3. Sew the long side of (1) Fabric 5 HST to the long side of (1) Fabric 1 HST as shown to make a 3½" x 3½" 5-1 HST. Press seam to Fabric 5. Make 32.

 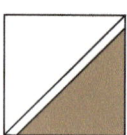 

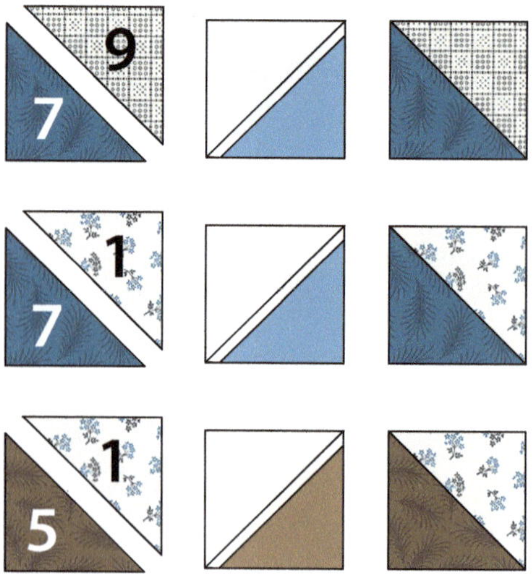

4. Sew the long side of (1) Fabric 3 HST to the long side of (1) Fabric 9 HST as shown to make a 3½" x 3½" 3-9 HST. Press seam to Fabric 3. Make 32.

  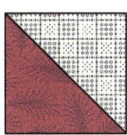

5. Lay out all of the HSTs in 4 rows of 4 HSTs each as shown, noting the orientation of each unit.

6. Sew the HSTs together in each row. Join the rows to make a 12½" x 12½" Anna's Affection block. Clip, swirl and press seams as necessary to achieve a flat seam. Make 8 blocks.

Team Cora

Anna's Affection

Make 8

Team Carson

Team Rose

To continue your adventure,
JUMP TO PAGE 49

Sarah's Daring

Make 8

Finished Block Size: 12" x 12"
Unfinished Block Size: 12½" x 12½"

Cutting

Color #	Team Cora	Team Carson	Team Rose	Cutting
1	A-7598-R	A-7597-B	A-7614-EC	Cut (4) 3⅞" x WOF strips. From this, cut (32) 3⅞" squares. Cut along one diagonal for (64) HSTs. [HST-3]
3	A-7330-ET	A-7332-R	A-7616-EG	Cut (2) 3⅞" x WOF strips. From this, cut (16) 3⅞" squares. Cut along one diagonal for (32) HSTs. [HST-3]
5	A-7332-R	A-7332-N	A-7615-E	Cut (2) 3⅞" x WOF strips. From this, cut (16) 3⅞" squares. Cut along one diagonal for (32) HSTs. [HST-3]
7	A-7665-B	A-7332-B1	A-7615-B	Cut (4) 3⅞" x WOF strips. From this, cut (32) 3⅞" squares. Cut along one diagonal for (64) HSTs. [HST-3]
9	A-7597-G	A-7602-K	A-7597-R	Cut (4) 3⅞" x WOF strips. From this, cut (32) 3⅞" squares. Cut along one diagonal for (64) HSTs. [HST-3]

Assembly

1. Sew the long side of (1) Fabric 5 HST to the long side of (1) Fabric 9 HST as shown to make a 3½" x 3½" 5-9 HST. Press seam to Fabric 5. Make 32.

2. Sew the long side of (1) Fabric 7 HST to the long side of (1) Fabric 1 HST as shown to make a 3½" x 3½" 7-1 HST. Press seam to Fabric 7. Make 64.

3. Sew the long side of (1) Fabric 3 HST to the long side of (1) Fabric 9 HST as shown to make a 3½" x 3½" 3-9 HST. Press seam to Fabric 3. Make 32.

 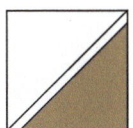 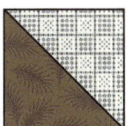
 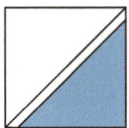 
 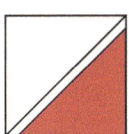 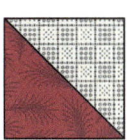

4. Lay out all of the HSTs in 4 rows of 4 HSTs each as shown, noting the orientation of each unit.

5. Sew the HSTs together in each row. Join the rows to make a 12½" x 12½" Sarah's Daring block. Clip, swirl and press seams as necessary to achieve a flat seam. Make 8 blocks.

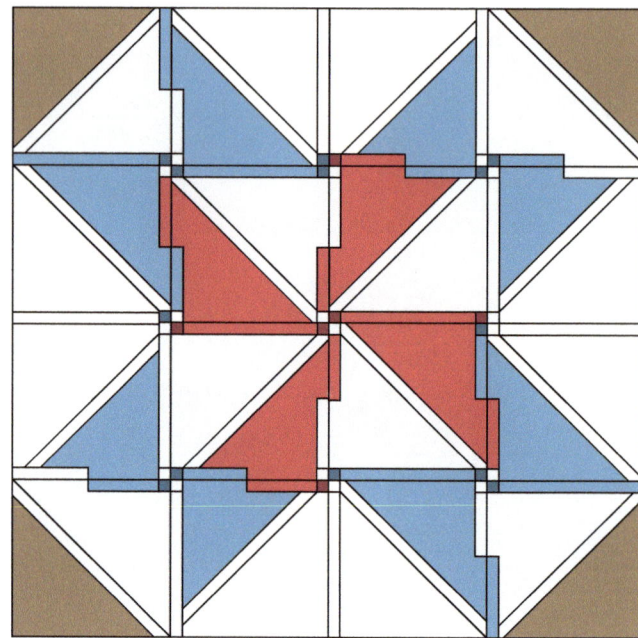

Team Cora

Sarah's Daring

Make 8

Team Carson

Team Rose

To continue your adventure,
JUMP TO PAGE 49

Confidante Medley

Anna's Affection – MAKE 4 | *Sarah's Daring* – MAKE 4

Finished Block Size: 12" x 12"
Unfinished Block Size: 12½" x 12½"

Cutting

Color #	Team Cora	Team Carson	Team Rose	Cutting
1	A-7598-R	A-7597-B	A-7614-EC	Cut (4) 3⅞" x WOF strips. From this, cut (32) 3⅞" squares. Cut along one diagonal for (64) HSTs. [HST-3]
3	A-7330-ET	A-7332-R	A-7616-EG	Cut (2) 3⅞" x WOF strips. From this, cut (16) 3⅞" squares. Cut along one diagonal for (32) HSTs. [HST-3]
5	A-7332-R	A-7332-N	A-7615-E	Cut (2) 3⅞" x WOF strips. From this, cut (16) 3⅞" squares. Cut along one diagonal for (32) HSTs. [HST-3]
7	A-7665-B	A-7332-B1	A-7615-B	Cut (4) 3⅞" x WOF strips. From this, cut (32) 3⅞" squares. Cut along one diagonal for (64) HSTs. [HST-3]
9	A-7597-G	A-7602-K	A-7597-R	Cut (4) 3⅞" x WOF strips. From this, cut (32) 3⅞" squares. Cut along one diagonal for (64) HSTs. [HST-3]

Anna's Affection
[MAKE 4]

Assembly

1. Sew the long side of (1) Fabric 7 HST to the long side of (1) Fabric 9 HST as shown to make a 3½" x 3½" 7-9 HST. Press seam to Fabric 7. Make 16.

2. Sew the long side of (1) Fabric 7 HST to the long side of (1) Fabric 1 HST as shown to make a 3½" x 3½" 7-1 HST. Press seam to Fabric 7. Make 16.

 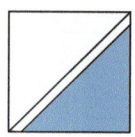 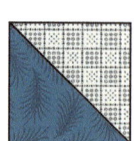
 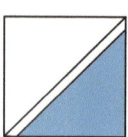 

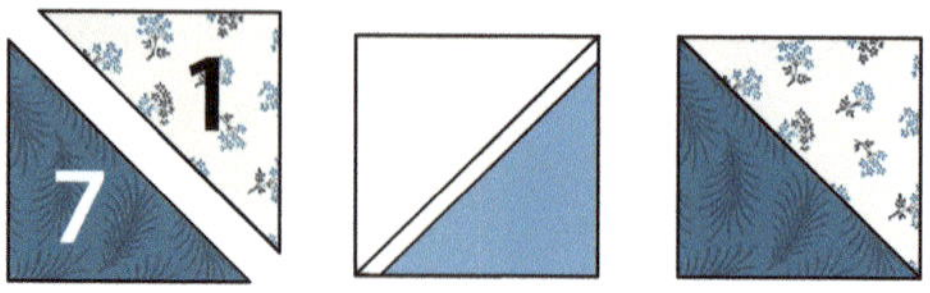

3. Sew the long side of (1) Fabric 5 HST to the long side of (1) Fabric 1 HST as shown to make a 3½" x 3½" 5-1 HST. Press seam to Fabric 5. Make 16.

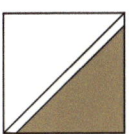 

4. Sew the long side of (1) Fabric 3 HST to the long side of (1) Fabric 9 HST as shown to make a 3½" x 3½" 3-9 HST. Press seam to Fabric 3. Make 16.

 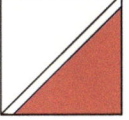 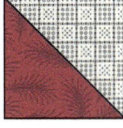

5. Lay out all of the HSTs in 4 rows of 4 HSTs each as shown, noting the orientation of each unit.

6. Sew the HSTs together in each row. Join the rows to make a 12½" x 12½" Anna's Affection block. Clip, swirl and press seams as necessary to achieve a flat seam. Make 4 blocks.

English Manor Mystery Quilt Along ❖ **Confidante, Week 3**

Anna's Affection

Make 4

Team Cora

Team Carson

Team Rose

Continue to next page ▶

Sarah's Daring

[Make 4]

Assembly

  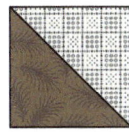

 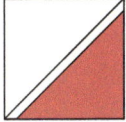 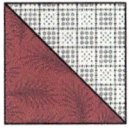

1. Sew the long side of (1) Fabric 5 HST to the long side of (1) Fabric 9 HST as shown to make a 3½" x 3½" 5-9 HST. Press seam to Fabric 5. Make 16.

2. Sew the long side of (1) Fabric 7 HST to the long side of (1) Fabric 1 HST as shown to make a 3½" x 3½" 7-1 HST. Press seam to Fabric 7. Make 32.

3. Sew the long side of (1) Fabric 3 HST to the long side of (1) Fabric 9 HST as shown to make a 3½" x 3½" 3-9 HST. Press seam to Fabric 3. Make 16.

4. Lay out all of the HSTs in 4 rows of 4 HSTs each as shown, noting the orientation of each unit.

5. Sew the HSTs together in each row. Join the rows to make a 12½" x 12½" Sarah's Daring block. Clip, swirl and press seams as necessary to achieve a flat seam. Make 4 blocks.

 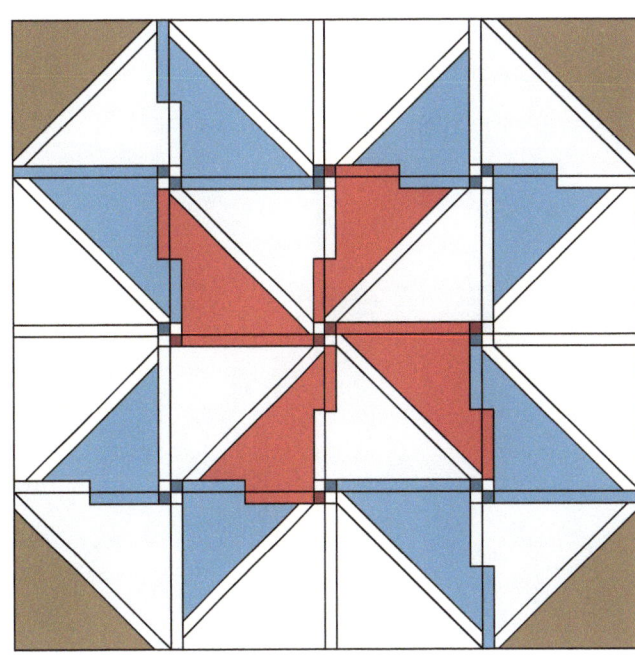

Team Cora

Sarah's Daring

Make 4

Team Carson

Team Rose

TO CONTINUE YOUR ADVENTURE,
READ THE NEXT PAGE ▶

Attendant
Week Four

A Gift from a Stranger...

The nearer lady's maid discreetly hands you something from behind her back. "It's from one of the dinner guests. He heard you were going to be arriving today, and wanted to send you something special to complete your outfit."

It's so perfect—a small bunch of white hydrangeas (presumably from the White Border Garden along the castle lane) that you take in delight. You thank her for bringing you the gift and ask who it's from. "You'll find out at dinner," she says coyly, and takes her leave.

You've traveled down the hallways of this castle so often over the past four years that you know the way to the dining room easily. On your way down, you're surprised not to encounter any of the other residents along the way—but of course, they'll all be waiting for you.

As you enter the dining room, you're surprised—no, shocked—to learn the identity of the gift-giving dinner guest. Why, it's Julian Fellowes! "Julian! What are you doing here?" you exclaim.

"I'd like to ask you the same question," he retorts. "You've come in through the wrong door and now you're blocking my shot."

Apparently you don't know the halls as well as you thought, and since this development isn't any stranger than what's happened up to now, you turn around without a word and approach the dining room from the opposite door. "Excellent! Cut!" Julian gleefully announces. "That's a wrap folks!"

"What about dinner?" you ask. "Oh, it wasn't a real dinner we needed you for; just background. You may go," he says dismissively. "Thomas or Bates can walk you back to your estate."

If you ask Thomas Barrow to walk you back, go to Thomas's Clock, page 50.
If you ask John Bates to walk you back, go to John's Loyalty, page 52.
If you ask them both to walk you back, go to Attendant Medley, page 54.

Thomas's Clock
GO TO PAGE **50**

John's Loyalty
GO TO PAGE **52**

Attendant Medley
GO TO PAGE **54**

Thomas's Clock

MAKE 16

Finished Block Size: 6" x 6"
Unfinished Block Size: 6½" x 6½"

Cutting

Color #	Team Cora	Team Carson	Team Rose	Cutting
7	A-7665-B	A-7332-B1	A-7615-B	Cut (2) 3⅞" x WOF strips. From this, cut (16) 3⅞" squares. Cut along one diagonal for (32) HSTs. [HST-3]
8	A-7665-R	A-7666-BN	A-7616-BP	Cut (2) 3⅞" x WOF strips. From this, cut (16) 3⅞" squares. Cut along one diagonal for (32) HSTs. [HST-3]
10	A-7598-N	A-7601-G	A-7598-N	Cut (2) 4¾" x WOF strips. From this, cut (16) 4¾" squares. [SOP-6]

Assembly

1. Sew the long side of (2) Fabric 7 HSTs to opposite sides of (1) 4¾" Fabric 10 square. Press seams open.

2. Sew the long side of (2) Fabric 8 HSTs to the remaining sides of the Fabric 10 square. Press seams open to make a 6½" x 6½" Thomas's Clock block. Make 16 blocks.

 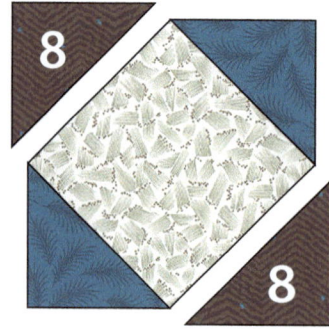 

Thomas's Clock

Make 16

Team Cora

Team Carson

Team Rose

TO CONTINUE YOUR ADVENTURE,
JUMP TO PAGE 59

John's Loyalty
Make 16

Finished Block Size: 6" x 6"
Unfinished Block Size: 6½" x 6½"

Cutting

Color #	Team Cora	Team Carson	Team Rose	Cutting
7	A-7665-B	A-7332-B1	A-7615-B	Cut (1) 7¼" x WOF strip. From this, cut (4) 7¼" squares. Cut along both diagonals for (16) QSTs. [QST-6]
8	A-7665-R	A-7666-BN	A-7616-BP	Cut (1) 7¼" x WOF strip. From this, cut (4) 7¼" squares. Cut along both diagonals for (16) QSTs. [QST-6]
10	A-7598-N	A-7601-G	A-7598-N	Cut (4) 3⅞" x WOF strips. From this, cut (32) 3⅞" squares. Cut along one diagonal for (64) HSTs. [HST-3]

Assembly

1. Sew the long side of (1) Fabric 10 HST to the short side of (1) Fabric 7 QST as shown. Press seam open.

2. Sew the long side of a second Fabric 10 HST to the adjacent short side of the Fabric 7 QST to make a 10-7 flying geese unit. Press seam open. Make 16.

  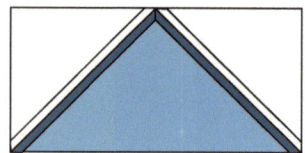

3. Sew the long side of (1) Fabric 10 HST to the short side of (1) Fabric 8 QST as shown. Press seam open.

4. Sew the long side of a second Fabric 10 HST to the adjacent short side of the Fabric 8 QST to make a 10-8 flying geese unit. Press seam open. Make 16.

 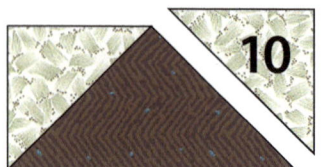 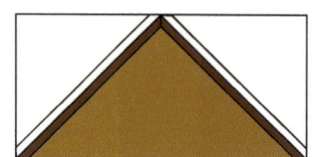

5. Sew (1) 10-7 flying geese unit to (1) 10-8 flying geese unit to make a 6½" x 6½" John's Loyalty block. Clip and press seams as necessary to achieve a flat seam. Make 16 blocks.

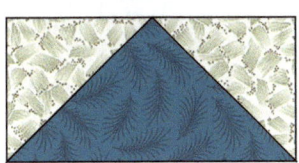
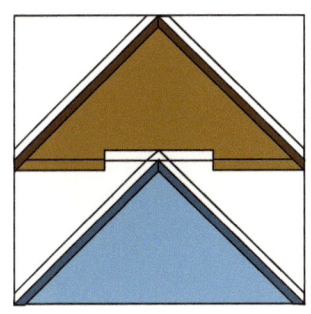

John's Loyalty

Make 16

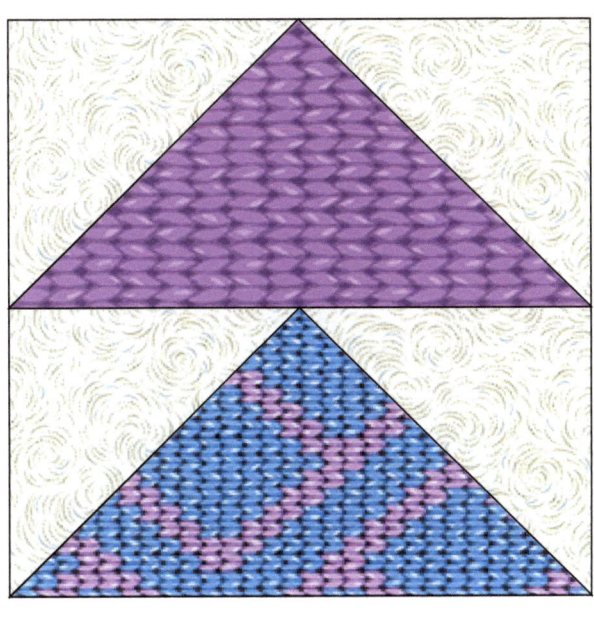

Team Cora

Team Carson

Team Rose

TO CONTINUE YOUR ADVENTURE,
JUMP TO PAGE 59

Attendant Medley

Thomas's Clock – MAKE 8 | *John's Loyalty* – MAKE 8

Finished Block Size: 6" x 6"
Unfinished Block Size: 6½" x 6½"

Cutting

Color #	Team Cora	Team Carson	Team Rose	Cutting
7	A-7665-B	A-7332-B1	A-7615-B	Cut (1) 8" x WOF strip. From this, cut (2) 8" x 16" rectangles. From (1) 8" x 16" rectangle, cut (8) 3⅞" squares. Cut along one diagonal for (16) HSTs. [HST-3] From remaining 8" x 16" rectangle, cut (2) 7¼" squares. Cut along both diagonals for (8) QSTs. [QST-6]
8	A-7665-R	A-7666-BN	A-7616-BP	Cut (1) 8" x WOF strip. From this, cut (2) 8" x 16" rectangles. From (1) 8" x 16" rectangle, cut (8) 3⅞" squares. Cut along one diagonal for (16) HSTs. [HST-3] From remaining 8" x 16" rectangle, cut (2) 7¼" squares. Cut along both diagonals for (8) QSTs. [QST-6]]
10	A-7598-N	A-7601-G	A-7598-N	Cut (2) 3⅞" x WOF strips. From this, cut (16) 3⅞" squares. Cut along one diagonal for (32) HSTs. [HST-3] Cut (1) 4¾" x WOF strip. From this, cut (8) 4¾" squares. [SOP-6]

Thomas's Clock

[MAKE 8]

Assembly

1. Sew the long side of (2) Fabric 7 HSTs to opposite sides of (1) 4¾" Fabric 10 square. Press seams open.

2. Sew the long side of (2) Fabric 8 HSTs to the remaining sides of the Fabric 10 square. Press seams open to make a 6½" x 6½" Thomas's Clock block. Make 8 blocks.

 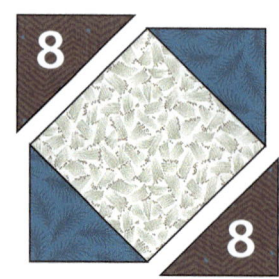 

Thomas's Clock

Make 8

Team Cora

Team Carson

Team Rose

Continue to next page ▶

John's Loyalty
[Make 8]

Assembly

1. Sew the long side of (1) Fabric 10 HST to the short side of (1) Fabric 7 QST as shown. Press seam open.

2. Sew the long side of a second Fabric 10 HST to the adjacent short side of the Fabric 7 QST to make a 10-7 flying geese unit. Press seam open. Make 8.

  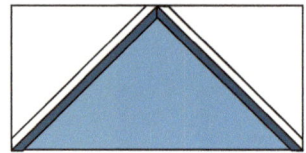

3. Sew the long side of (1) Fabric 10 HST to the short side of (1) Fabric 8 QST as shown. Press seam open.

4. Sew the long side of a second Fabric 10 HST to the adjacent short side of the Fabric 8 QST to make a 10-8 flying geese unit. Press seam open. Make 8.

  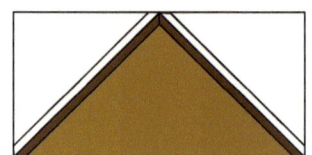

5. Sew (1) 10-7 flying geese unit to (1) 10-8 flying geese unit to make a 6½" x 6½" John's Loyalty block. Clip and press seams as necessary to achieve a flat seam. Make 8 blocks.

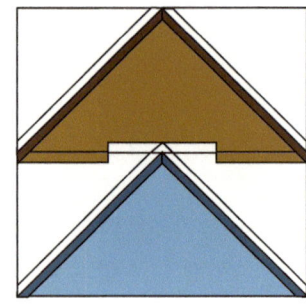

John's Loyalty

Make 8

Team Cora

Team Carson

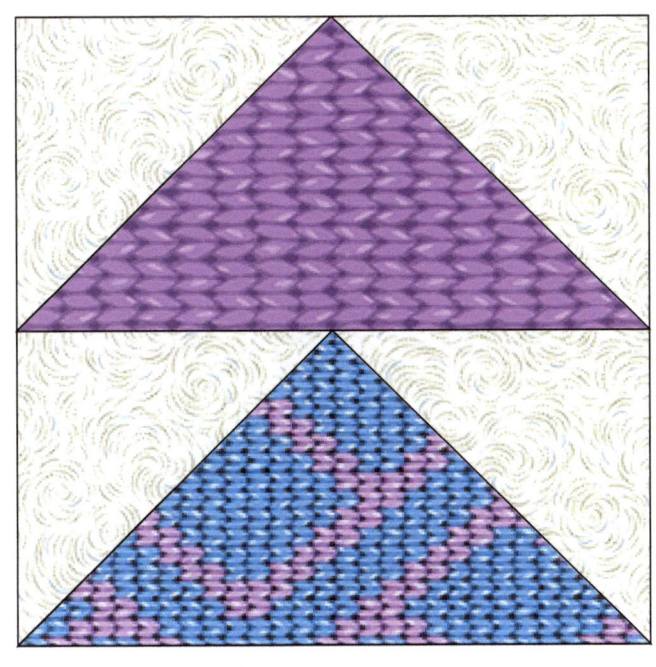

Team Rose

TO CONTINUE YOUR ADVENTURE,
JUMP TO PAGE 59

Don't Miss the Most Anticipated Quilting Event since the Downton Abbey Quilt Alongs!

Dear Laura

LITTLE HOUSE ON THE PRAIRIE
Mystery Quilt Along

Registration opens on September 6th.
The fun begins January 10, 2016.

With our online classes, you're never too late to the party! Your access never expires, and you'll get instant access to videos, full-color photo tutorials, and our exclusive website Forum for additional support.

http://eLBS.us/DL

Culinarian
Week Five

Never Miss a Good Pudding...

The walk back is pleasant enough, but after a few minutes you realize you have no idea where you are going. You ask your walking partner, "How do you know where my estate is located when I don't?"

They reply, "The village is quite small. We know everyone! Don't worry; we are almost there."

After a few more minutes of awkward silence (for what on earth do you say to a famous actor or a servant - ask how their day went?) you spot a lovely little cottage up ahead, with smoke tendrils climbing from the chimney. "Oh, who lives in that adorable little house?" you ask.

"You do," is the reply.

You stop short with a puzzled look on your face and turn your head back and forth from your attendant to the house and back to the attendant. "Pardon me," you say, as you break into a giddy run across the green. So this is the estate! It isn't at all like you pictured, but it looks quite lovely all the same. It reminds you a bit of your own house back home.

As you approach the house, you smell the aroma of chicken, and biscuits, and… pudding! It would be such a pity to miss a good pudding. You fling open the door, and sprint down the hall; you're pretty sure you know who's in the kitchen already…

If Daisy is in the kitchen, go to Sous Chef Daisy, page 60.
If Mrs. Patmore is in the kitchen, go to Master Chef Beryl, page 63.
If they are both in the kitchen, go to Culinarian Medley, page 66.

Sous Chef Daisy
GO TO PAGE **60**

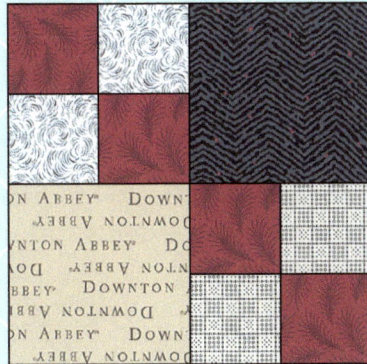

Master Chef Beryl
GO TO PAGE **63**

Culinarian Medley
GO TO PAGE **66**

Sous Chef Daisy
MAKE 16

Finished Block Size: 8" x 8"
Unfinished Block Size: 8½" x 8½"

Cutting

Color #	Team Cora	Team Carson	Team Rose	Cutting
2	 A-7332-K1	 A-7666-RK	 A-7332-B1	Cut a 4⅞" x WOF strip. From this, cut (8) 4⅞" squares. Cut along one diagonal for (16) HSTs. [HST-4] Cut a 2½" x WOF strip. From this, cut (16) 2½" squares. [SQ-2]
3	 A-7330-ET	 A-7332-R	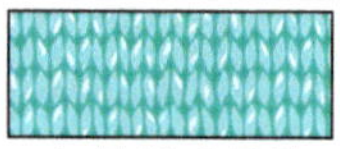 A-7616-EG	Cut (2) 2½" x WOF strips. From this, cut (32) 2½" squares. [SQ-2]
4	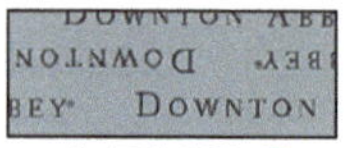 A-7617-C	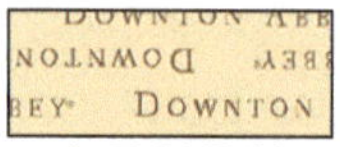 A-7617-N	 A-7613-E	Cut a 4⅞" x WOF strip. From this, cut (8) 4⅞" squares. Cut along one diagonal for (16) HSTs. [HST-4] Cut a 2½" x WOF strip. From this, cut (16) 2½" squares. [SQ-2]
6	 A-7598-B	 A-7598-B	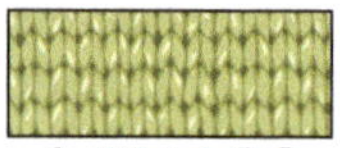 A-7616-BG	Cut (4) 2½" x WOF strips. From this, cut (64) 2½" squares. [SQ-2]
9	 A-7597-G	 A-7602-K	 A-7597-R	Cut (2) 4⅞" x WOF strip. From this, cut (16) 4⅞" squares. Cut along one diagonal for (32) HSTs. [HST-4]

Assembly

1. Sew (1) Fabric 3 SQ-2 to (1) Fabric 6 SQ-2 to make a 2½" x 4½" 3-6 two-patch unit. Press seam to Fabric 3. Make 32.

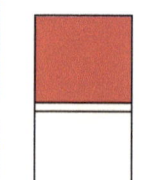

2. Sew (1) Fabric 2 SQ-2 to (1) Fabric 6 SQ-2 to make a 2½" x 4½" 2-6 two-patch unit. Press seam to Fabric 2. Make 16.

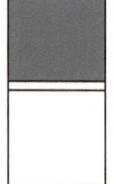

3. Sew (1) Fabric 4 SQ-2 to (1) Fabric 6 SQ-2 to make a 2½" x 4½" 4-6 two-patch unit. Press seam to Fabric 4. Make 16.

4. Sew (1) 3-6 unit to (1) 2-6 unit with the Fabric 6 squares opposite each other as shown to make a 4½" x 4½" 3-2-6 four-patch square. Clip, swirl and press seams as necessary to achieve a flat seam. Make 16.

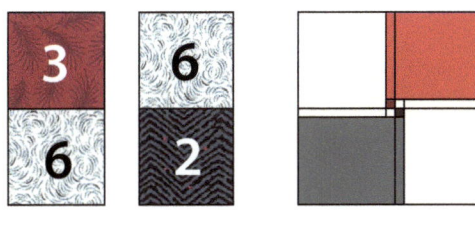

5. Sew (1) 3-6 unit to (1) 4-6 unit with the Fabric 6 squares opposite each other as shown to make a 4½" x 4½" 3-4-6 four-patch square. Clip, swirl and press seams as necessary to achieve a flat seam. Make 16.

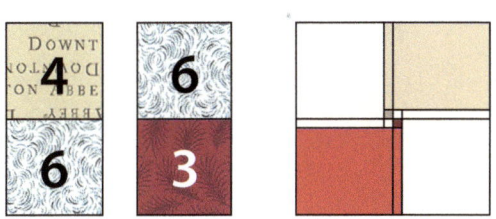

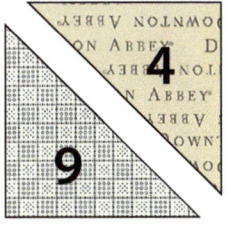
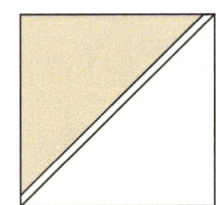

6. Sew (1) Fabric 4 HST-4 to (1) Fabric 9 HST-4 to make a 4½" x 4½" 4-9 HST unit. Press seam to Fabric 4. Make 16.

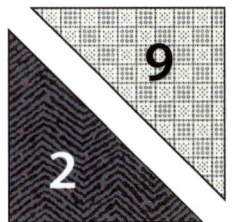
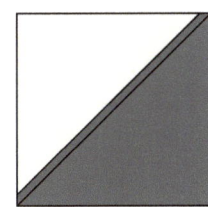

7. Sew (1) Fabric 2 HST-4 to (1) Fabric 9 HST-4 to make a 4½" x 4½" 2-9 HST unit. Press seam to Fabric 2. Make 16.

8. Sew (1) 3-2-6 four-patch square to (1) 4-9 HST unit to make block row one. Press seam to the 4-9 HST.

9. Sew (1) 3-4-6 four-patch square to (1) 2-9 HST unit to make block row two. Press seam to the 2-9 HST.

10. Sew block row one to the top of block row two, with the four-patch squares opposite each other, to make an 8½" x 8½" Sous Chef Daisy block. Clip, swirl and press seams as necessary to achieve a flat seam. Make 16 blocks.

English Manor Mystery Quilt Along ❖ Culinarian, Week 5

Team Cora

Sous Chef Daisy

Make 16

Team Carson

Team Rose

TO CONTINUE YOUR ADVENTURE,
JUMP TO PAGE 71

Master Chef Beryl
Make 16

Finished Block Size: 8" x 8"
Unfinished Block Size: 8½" x 8½"

Cutting

Color #	Team Cora	Team Carson	Team Rose	Cutting
2	A-7332-K1	A-7666-RK	A-7332-B1	Cut (2) 4½" x WOF strips. From this, cut (16) 4½" squares. [SQ-4]
3	A-7330-ET	A-7332-R	A-7616-EG	Cut (4) 2½" x WOF strips. From this, cut (64) 2½" squares. [SQ-2]
4	A-7617-C	A-7617-N	A-7613-E	Cut (2) 4½" x WOF strips. From this, cut (16) 4½" squares. [SQ-4]
6	A-7598-B	A-7598-B	A-7616-BG	Cut (2) 2½" x WOF strips. From this, cut (32) 2½" squares. [SQ-2]
9	A-7597-G	A-7602-K	A-7597-R	Cut (2) 2½" x WOF strips. From this, cut (32) 2½" squares. [SQ-2]

Assembly

1. Sew (1) Fabric 3 SQ-2 to (1) Fabric 6 SQ-2 to make a 2½" x 4½" 3-6 two-patch unit. Press seam to Fabric 3. Make 32.

2. Sew (1) Fabric 3 SQ-2 to (1) Fabric 9 SQ-2 to make a 2½" x 4½" 3-9 two-patch unit. Press seam to Fabric 3. Make 32.

3. Sew (1) 3-6 unit to a second 3-6 unit with the Fabric 6 squares opposite each other as shown to make a 4½" x 4½" 3-6 four-patch square. Clip, swirl and press seams as necessary to achieve a flat seam. Make 16.

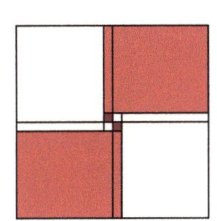

4. Sew (1) 3-9 unit to a second 3-9 unit with the Fabric 9 squares opposite each other as shown to make a 4½" x 4½" 3-9 four-patch square. Clip, swirl and press seams as necessary to achieve a flat seam. Make 16.

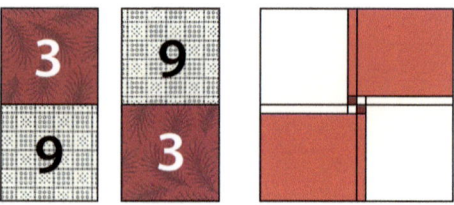

5. Sew (1) 3-6 four-patch square to (1) Fabric 2 SQ-4 to make block row one. Press seam to Fabric 2.

6. Sew (1) 3-9 four-patch square to (1) Fabric 4 SQ-4 to make block row two. Press seam to Fabric 4.

7. Sew block row one to the top of block row two, with the four-patch squares opposite each other, to make an 8½" x 8½" Master Chef Beryl block. Clip, swirl and press seams as necessary to achieve a flat seam. Make 16 blocks.

Master Chef Beryl

Make 16

Team Cora

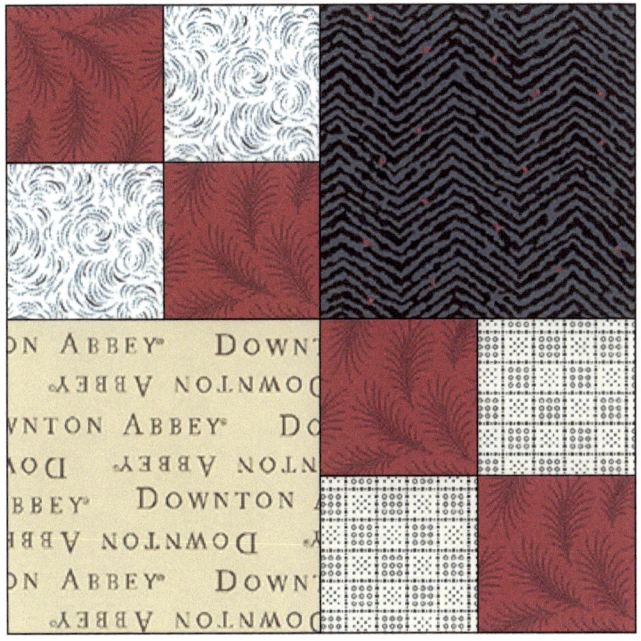

Team Carson

Team Rose

TO CONTINUE YOUR ADVENTURE,
JUMP TO PAGE 71

Culinarian Medley

Sous Chef Daisy – MAKE 8 | Master Chef Beryl – MAKE 8

Finished Block Size: 8" x 8"
Unfinished Block Size: 8½" x 8½"

Cutting

Color #	Team Cora	Team Carson	Team Rose	Cutting
2	A-7332-K1	A-7666-RK	A-7332-B1	Cut a 4½" x WOF strip. From this, cut (8) 4½" squares. [SQ-4] Cut a 5" x WOF strip. From this, cut (2) 5" x 20" strips: From (1) 5" x 20" strip, cut (4) 4⅞" squares. Cut across one diagonal for (8) HSTs. [HST-4] From (1) 5" x 20" strip, cut (8) 2½" squares. [SQ-2]
3	A-7330-ET	A-7332-R	A-7616-EG	Cut (3) 2½" x WOF strips. From this, cut (48) 2½" squares. [SQ-2]
4	A-7617-C	A-7617-N	A-7613-E	Cut a 4½" x WOF strip. From this, cut (8) 4½" squares. [SQ-4] Cut a 5" x WOF strip. From this, cut (2) 5" x 20" strips: From (1) 5" x 20" strip, cut (4) 4⅞" squares. Cut across one diagonal for (8) HSTs. [HST-4] From (1) 5" x 20" strip, cut (8) 2½" squares. [SQ-2]
6	A-7598-B	A-7598-B	A-7616-BG	Cut (3) 2½" x WOF strips. From this, cut (48) 2½" squares. [SQ-2]
9	A-7597-G	A-7602-K	A-7597-R	Cut (1) 4⅞" x WOF strip. From this, cut (8) 4⅞" squares. Cut along one diagonal for (16) HSTs. [HST-4] Cut (1) 2½" x WOF strip. From this, cut (16) 2½" squares. [SQ-2]

Sous Chef Daisy
[MAKE 8]

Assembly

1. Sew (1) Fabric 3 SQ-2 to (1) Fabric 6 SQ-2 to make a 2½" x 4½" 3-6 two-patch unit. Press seam to Fabric 3. Make 16.

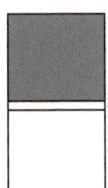

2. Sew (1) Fabric 2 SQ-2 to (1) Fabric 6 SQ-2 to make a 2½" x 4½" 2-6 two-patch unit. Press seam to Fabric 2. Make 8.

3. Sew (1) Fabric 4 SQ-2 to (1) Fabric 6 SQ-2 to make a 2½" x 4½" 4-6 two-patch unit. Press seam to Fabric 4. Make 8.

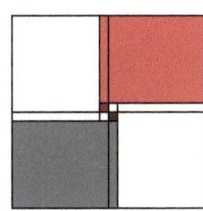

4. Sew (1) 3-6 unit to (1) 2-6 unit with the Fabric 6 squares opposite each other as shown to make a 4½" x 4½" 3-2-6 four-patch square. Clip, swirl and press seams as necessary to achieve a flat seam. Make 8.

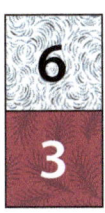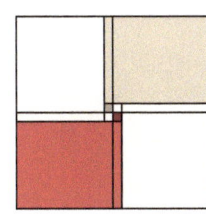

5. Sew (1) 3-6 unit to (1) 4-6 unit with the Fabric 6 squares opposite each other as shown to make a 4½" x 4½" 3-4-6 four-patch square. Clip, swirl and press seams as necessary to achieve a flat seam. Make 8.

6. Sew (1) Fabric 4 HST-4 to (1) Fabric 9 HST-4 to make a 4½" x 4½" 4-9 HST unit. Press seam to Fabric 4. Make 8.

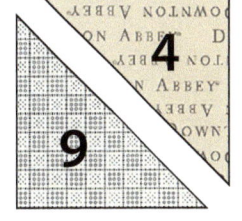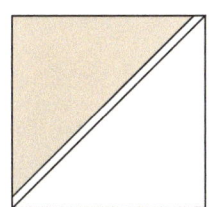

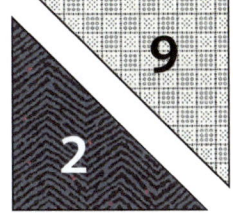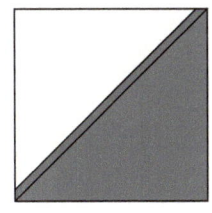

7. Sew (1) Fabric 2 HST-4 to (1) Fabric 9 HST-4 to make a 4½" x 4½" 2-9 HST unit. Press seam to Fabric 2. Make 8.

8. Sew (1) 3-2-6 four-patch square to (1) 4-9 HST unit to make block row one. Press seam to the 4-9 HST.

9. Sew (1) 3-4-6 four-patch square to (1) 2-9 HST unit to make block row two. Press seam to the 2-9 HST.

10. Sew block row one to the top of block row two, with the four-patch squares opposite each other, to make an 8½" x 8½" Sous Chef Daisy block. Clip, swirl and press seams as necessary to achieve a flat seam. Make 8 blocks.

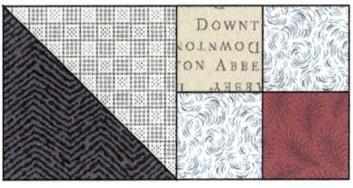

Team Cora

Sous Chef Daisy

Make 8

Team Carson

Team Rose

CONTINUE TO NEXT PAGE ▶

Master Chef Beryl
[Make 8]

Assembly

1. Sew (1) Fabric 3 SQ-2 to (1) Fabric 6 SQ-2 to make a 2½" x 4½" 3-6 two-patch unit. Press seam to Fabric 3. Make 16.

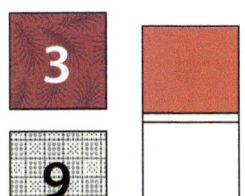

2. Sew (1) Fabric 3 SQ-2 to (1) Fabric 9 SQ-2 to make a 2½" x 4½" 3-9 two-patch unit. Press seam to Fabric 3. Make 16.

3. Sew (1) 3-6 unit to a second 3-6 unit with the Fabric 6 squares opposite each other as shown to make a 4½" x 4½" 3-6 four-patch square. Clip, swirl and press seams as necessary to achieve a flat seam. Make 8.

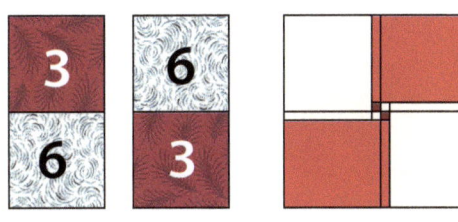

4. Sew (1) 3-9 unit to a second 3-9 unit with the Fabric 9 squares opposite each other as shown to make a 4½" x 4½" 3-9 four-patch square. Clip, swirl and press seams as necessary to achieve a flat seam. Make 8.

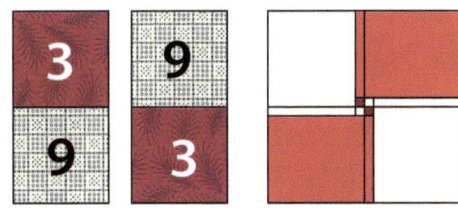

5. Sew (1) 3-6 four-patch square to (1) Fabric 2 SQ-4 to make block row one. Press seam to Fabric 2.

6. Sew (1) 3-9 four-patch square to (1) Fabric 4 SQ-4 to make block row two. Press seam to Fabric 4.

7. Sew block row one to the top of block row two, with the four-patch squares opposite each other, to make an 8½" x 8½" Master Chef Beryl block. Clip, swirl and press seams as necessary to achieve a flat seam. Make 8 blocks.

Team Cora

Master Chef Beryl

Make 8

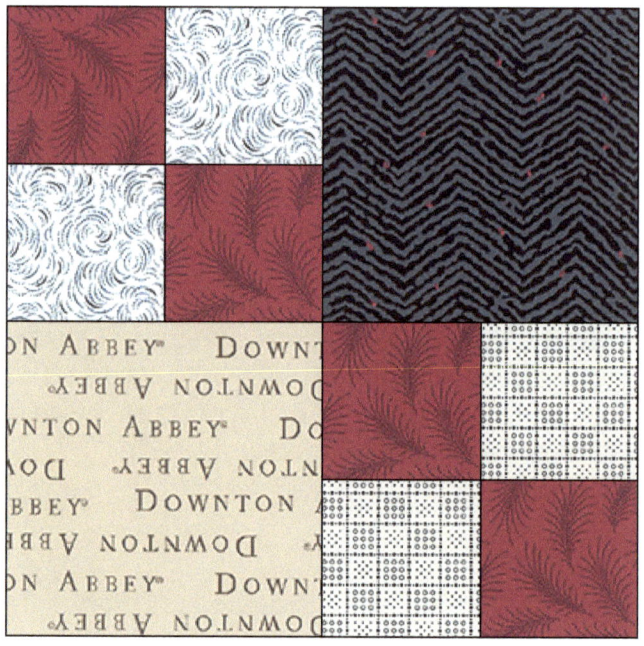

Team Carson

Team Rose

TO CONTINUE YOUR ADVENTURE,
READ THE NEXT PAGE ▶

Companion
Week Six

Mimosas for Everyone...

The feast you see before you is almost too fantastic to eat! There are so many fabulous meats, savory dishes, desserts and puddings (oh, the puddings!) that you stuff yourself within minutes. Oh, the chefs of the abbey are fine indeed.

"What are you doing here, at my house?" you inquire between bites.

"Julian thought it would be a good idea for us to feed you after your long journey," they explain. "And what better place to serve you dinner than in your own house?"

There's no arguing with that kind of logic, it seems. Now where is that pudding?

You locate the pudding on a table in the parlor. You serve yourself a heaping helping and drop into a chair. After only a couple of bites though, you yawn a great yawn, stretch, and decide a nap is in order. Because when one sits in a cozy chair by a fire after a huge meal, one must nap.

You wake up the next morning—stiff from your nap in the chair—to find the sun streaming in through the windows of the parlor. You must have been more tired than you thought. Someone at least thought to throw a quilt over you.

You hear the murmur of voices coming from another part of the house, so you go to seek them out. Oddly enough, you are startled to find someone you never expected to see in your dining room, serving up, of all things, mimosas.

**If the person in the dining room is Mrs. Painswick, go to Plucky Rosamund, page 72.
If the person in the dining room is Lady Rose, go to Energetic Rose, page 75.
If they are both in the dining room, go to Companion Medley, page 78.**

Plucky Rosamund
GO TO PAGE **72**

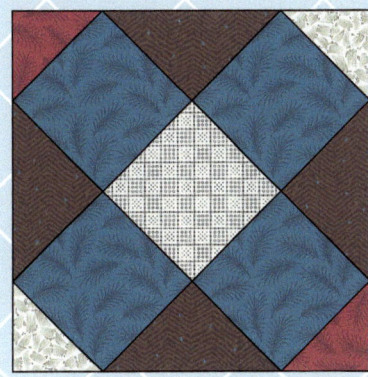

Energetic Rose
GO TO PAGE **75**

Companion Medley
GO TO PAGE **78**

Plucky Rosamund
MAKE 12

Finished Block Size: 12" x 12"
Unfinished Block Size: 12½" x 12½"

Cutting

Color #	Team Cora	Team Carson	Team Rose	Cutting
2	A-7332-K1	A-7666-RK	A-7332-B1	Cut (2) 5¼" x WOF strips. From this, cut (12) 5¼" squares. Cut along both diagonals for (48) QSTs. [QST-4]
3	A-7330-ET	A-7332-R	A-7616-EG	Cut (1) 5¼" x WOF strip. From this, cut (6) 5¼" squares. Cut along both diagonals for (24) QSTs. [QST-4]
7	A-7665-B	A-7332-B1	A-7615-B	Cut (6) 4⅞" x WOF strips. From this, cut (48) 4⅞" squares. Cut along one diagonal for (96) HSTs. [HST-4]
8	A-7665-R	A-7666-BN	A-7616-BP	Cut (3) 4⅞" x WOF strips. From this, cut (24) 4⅞" squares. Cut along one diagonal for (48) HSTs. [HST-4]
9	A-7597-G	A-7602-K	A-7597-R	Cut (2) 4½" x WOF strips. From this, cut (12) 4½" squares. [SQ-4]
10	A-7598-N	A-7601-G	A-7598-N	Cut (1) 5¼" x WOF strip. From this, cut (6) 5¼" squares. Cut along both diagonals for (24) QSTs. [QST-4]

Assembly

1. Sew (1) Fabric 3 QST to (1) Fabric 2 QST as shown to make a 3-2 HST. Press seam open. Make 24.

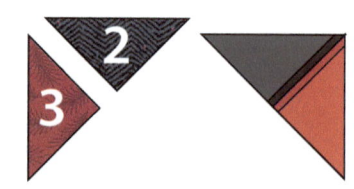

2. Sew (1) 3-2 HST to (1) Fabric 7 HST to make a 4½" x 4½" 3-2-7 square. Press seam to Fabric 7 HST. Make 24.

3. Sew (1) Fabric 10 QST to (1) Fabric 2 QST as shown to make a 10-2 HST. Press seam open. Make 24.

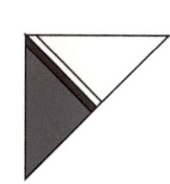

4. Sew (1) 10-2 HST to (1) Fabric 7 HST to make a 4½" x 4½" 10-2-7 square. Press seam to Fabric 7 HST. Make 24.

 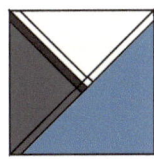

5. Sew (1) Fabric 8 HST to (1) Fabric 7 HST to make a 4½" x 4½" 8-7 square. Press seam open. Make 48.

6. Lay out (2) 3-2-7 squares, (2) 10-2-7 squares, (4) 8-7 squares and (1) Fabric 9 SQ in 3 rows of 3 squares each as shown.

7. Sew the squares together in each row. Press seams in the top and bottom rows to the 8-7 squares. Press seams in the center row to the Fabric 9 SQ.

8. Join the rows to make a 12½" x 12½" Plucky Rosamund block. Clip, swirl and press seams as necessary to achieve a flat seam. Make 12 blocks.

Team Cora

Plucky Rosamund

Make 12

Team Carson

Team Rose

To continue your adventure,
JUMP TO PAGE 83

Energetic Rose
Make 12

Finished Block Size: 12" x 12"
Unfinished Block Size: 12½" x 12½"

Cutting

Color #	Team Cora	Team Carson	Team Rose	Cutting
3	A-7330-ET	A-7332-R	A-7616-EG	Cut (2) 3⅞" x WOF strips. From this, cut (12) 3⅞" squares. Cut along one diagonal for (24) HSTs. [HST-3]
7	A-7665-B	A-7332-B1	A-7615-B	Cut (6) 4¾" x WOF strips. From this, cut (48) 4¾" squares. [SOP-6]
8	A-7665-R	A-7666-BN	A-7616-BP	Cut (3) 7¼" x WOF strips. From this, cut (12) 7¼" squares. Cut along both diagonals for (48) QSTs. [QST-6]
9	A-7597-G	A-7602-K	A-7597-R	Cut (2) 4¾" x WOF strips. From this, cut (12) 4¾" squares. [SOP-6]
10	A-7598-N	A-7601-G	A-7598-N	Cut (2) 3⅞" x WOF strips. From this, cut (12) 3⅞" squares. Cut along one diagonal for (24) HSTs. [HST-3]

Assembly

1. Sew (1) Fabric 7 square between (2) Fabric 8 QSTs as shown to make a top/bottom row. Press seams to the Fabric 8 QSTs. Make 24.

2. Sew (1) Fabric 9 square between (2) Fabric 7 squares as shown to make a center row. Press seams to the Fabric 9 square. Make 12.

3. Sew (1) center row between (2) top/bottom rows to make a nine-patch unit. Clip, swirl and press seams as necessary to achieve a flat seam.

4. Sew (2) Fabric 3 HSTs to opposite corners of the nine-patch unit. Press seams to Fabric 3 HSTs.

5. Sew (2) Fabric 10 HSTs to the remaining corners of the nine-patch unit. Press seams to Fabric 10 HSTs to complete a 12½" x 12½" Energetic Rose block. Make 12 blocks.

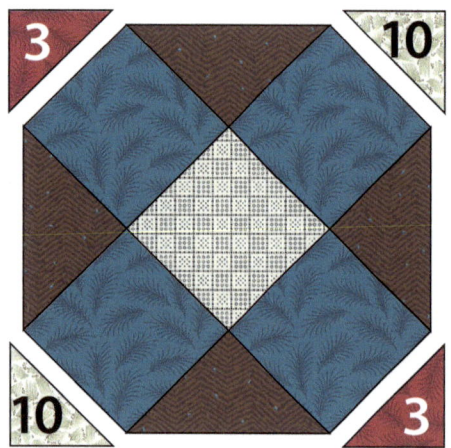

Team Cora

Energetic Rose

Make 12

Team Carson

Team Rose

TO CONTINUE YOUR ADVENTURE,
JUMP TO PAGE 83

Companion Medley

Plucky Rosamund– MAKE 6 | *Energetic Rose*– MAKE 6

Finished Block Size: 12" x 12"
Unfinished Block Size: 12½" x 12½"

Cutting

Color #	Team Cora	Team Carson	Team Rose	Cutting
2	 A-7332-K1	 A-7666-Rk	 A-7332-B1	Cut (1) 5¼" x WOF strip. From this, cut (6) 5¼" squares. Cut along both diagonals for (24) QSTs. [QST-4]
3	 A-7330-ET	 A-7332-R	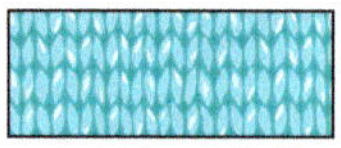 A-7616-EG	Cut (1) 5¼" x WOF strip. From this, cut (3) 5¼" squares. Cut along both diagonals for (12) QSTs. [QST-4] From remaining strip, cut (1) 3⅞" strip. From this, cut (6) 3⅞" squares. Cut along one diagonal for (12) HSTs. [HST-3]
7	 A-7665-B	 A-7332-B1	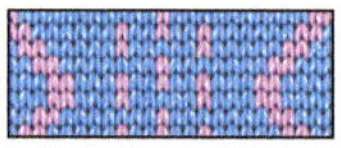 A-7615-B	Cut (3) 4⅞" x WOF strips. From this, cut (24) 4⅞" squares. Cut along one diagonal for (48) HSTs. [HST-4] Cut (3) 4¾" x WOF strips. From this, cut (24) 4¾" squares. [SOP-6]
8	 A-7665-R	 A-7666-BN	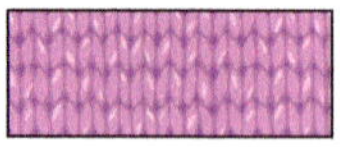 A-7616-BP	Cut (2) 4⅞" x WOF strips. From this, cut (12) 4⅞" squares. Cut along one diagonal for (24) HSTs. [HST-4] Cut (2) 7¼" x WOF strip. From this, cut (6) 7¼" squares. Cut along both diagonals for (24) QSTs. [QST-6]
9	 A-7597-G	 A-7602-K	 A-7597-R	Cut (1) 4½" x WOF strip. From this, cut (6) 4½" squares. [SQ-4] Cut (1) 4¾" x WOF strip. From this, cut (6) 4¾" squares. [SOP-6]
10	A-7598-N	 A-7601-G	A-7598-N	Cut (1) 5¼" x WOF strip. From this, cut (3) 5¼" squares. Cut along both diagonals for (12) QSTs. [QST-4] Cut (1) 3⅞" strip. From this, cut (6) 3⅞" squares. Cut along one diagonal for (12) HSTs. [HST-3]

Plucky Rosamund
[Make 6]

Assembly

1. Sew (1) Fabric 3 QST to (1) Fabric 2 QST as shown to make a 3-2 HST. Press seam open. Make 12.

2. Sew (1) 3-2 HST to (1) Fabric 7 HST to make a 4½" x 4½" 3-2-7 square. Press seam to Fabric 7 HST. Make 12.

 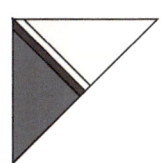

3. Sew (1) Fabric 10 QST to (1) Fabric 2 QST as shown to make a 10-2 HST. Press seam open. Make 12.

 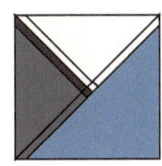

4. Sew (1) 10-2 HST to (1) Fabric 7 HST to make a 4½" x 4½" 10-2-7 square. Press seam to Fabric 7 HST. Make 12.

5. Sew (1) Fabric 8 HST to (1) Fabric 7 HST to make a 4½" x 4½" 8-7 square. Press seam open. Make 24.

6. Lay out (2) 3-2-7 squares, (2) 10-2-7 squares, (4) 8-7 squares and (1) 4½" Fabric 9 SQ in 3 rows of 3 squares each as shown.

7. Sew the squares together in each row. Press seams in the top and bottom rows to the 8-7 squares. Press seams in the center row to the 4½" Fabric 9 SQ.

8. Join the rows to make a 12½" x 12½" Plucky Rosamund block. Clip, swirl and press seams as necessary to achieve a flat seam. Make 6 blocks.

Team Cora

Plucky Rosamund

Make 6

Team Carson

Team Rose

CONTINUE TO NEXT PAGE ▶

Energetic Rose
[Make 6]

Assembly

1. Sew (1) Fabric 7 square between (2) Fabric 8 QSTs as shown to make a top/bottom row. Press seams to the Fabric 8 QSTs. Make 12.

2. Sew (1) 4¾" Fabric 9 square between (2) Fabric 7 squares as shown to make a center row. Press seams to the 4¾" Fabric 9 square. Make 6.

3. Sew (1) center row between (2) top/bottom rows to make a nine-patch unit. Clip, swirl and press seams as necessary to achieve a flat seam.

4. Sew (2) Fabric 3 HSTs to opposite corners of the nine-patch unit. Press seams to Fabric 3 HSTs.

5. Sew (2) Fabric 10 HSTs to the remaining corners of the nine-patch unit. Press seams to Fabric 10 HSTs to complete a 12½" x 12½" Energetic Rose block. Make 6 blocks.

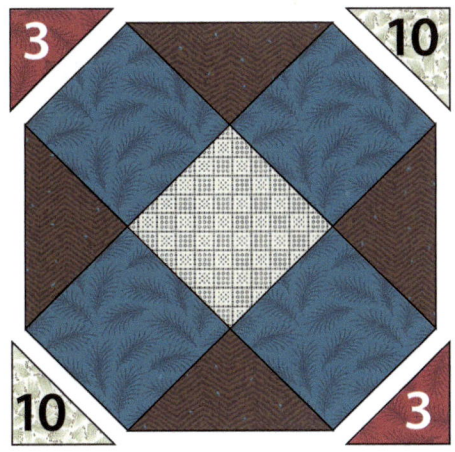

Team Cora

Energetic Rose

Make 6

Team Carson

Team Rose

To continue your adventure,
READ THE NEXT PAGE ▶

Finale
Week Seven

The Business of Life...

Not only are you being served a mimosa by a member of the extended Grantham clan, but there are many others there to enjoy mimosas too: Lord & Lady Grantham, Carson, Anna, O'Brien, Thomas, Bates, Daisy, Mrs. Patmore, Rosamund, and Rose. Even Julian is there, which you find a bit odd, but is by now something you are quite used to.

After all the mimosas are passed around, you call for a toast. Everyone starts pointing fingers at one another, but you have someone special in mind.

"Mr. Carson," you ask. "Will you do me the great honor of presenting the toast for this occasion?".

"Certainly," he replies. He clears his throat, and recites a fitting line from Season 4.
"The business of life is the acquisition of memories. In the end that's all there is."

"Hear, hear!" shouts everyone, and you all take a sip of your mimosas.

All of a sudden, while you're sipping your mimosa, you get a feeling of déjà vu. You start to feel a little woozy. Your vision starts to get grainy, and just before you pass out, you bid everyone farewell.

You wake up next to your sewing machine, surrounded by dozens of quilt blocks, and to the TV playing an episode of Downton Abbey. That will teach you to binge-watch Downton while you sew!

In the meantime, you've got all these blocks to put together into a quilt, and a mimosa sounds like just the thing to have before you dive in.

To assemble Manor House, Lady's Tiara, Anna's Affection, Thomas's Clock, Sous Chef Daisy and Plucky Rosamund, go to Finale One, page 84.
To assemble Manor House, Earl's Pipe, Sarah's Daring, John's Loyalty, Master Chef Beryl and Energetic Rose, go to Finale Two, page 90.
To assemble Manor House and the Medley Blocks, go to Finale Three, page 96.

Finale One
GO TO PAGE **84**

Finale Two
GO TO PAGE **90**

Finale Three
GO TO PAGE **96**

Finale One

Finished Quilt Size: 72" x 92"
Unfinished Quilt Size: 72½" x 92½"

Cutting

Color #	Team Cora	Team Carson	Team Rose	Cutting
2	A-7332-K1	A-7666-RK	A-7332-B1	Cut (6) 2½" x WOF strips. Piece strips end-to-end to make one long strip. From this, cut (2) 2½" x 48½" strips and (2) 2½" x 64½" strips.
3	A-7330-ET	A-7332-R	A-7616-EG	Cut (3) 2½" x WOF strips. From this, cut (2) 2½" x 20½" strips and (2) 2½" x 24½" strips. Cut (9) 2½" x WOF strips for binding.
5	A-7332-R	A-7332-N	A-7615-E	Cut (7) 2½" x WOF strips. Piece strips end-to-end to make one long strip. From this, cut (4) 2½" x 68½" strips.
Any	BACKING	BACKING	BACKING	5¾ yards
Any	BATTING	BATTING	BATTING	80" x 100"

Assembly
(Refer to the Finale One Quilt Assembly diagrams on pages 86, 87 and 88.)

1. Sew (2) 2½" x 20½" Fabric 3 strips to the top and bottom of the Week One: Manor House block. Press seams toward the Fabric 3 strips.

2. Sew (2) 2½" x 24½" Fabric 3 strips to the sides of the Week One: Manor House block to make a 24½" x 24½" quilt center. Press seams toward the Fabric 3 strips.

3. Sew (2) 12½" x 12½" Week Two: Lady's Tiara blocks together horizontally as shown to make a top/bottom border. Clip, swirl and press seams as necessary to achieve a flat seam. Make 2. Sew to the top and bottom of the quilt center.

4. Sew (4) 12½" x 12½" Week Three: Anna's Affection blocks together vertically as shown to make a side border. Clip, swirl and press seams as necessary to achieve a flat seam. Make 2. Sew to the sides of the quilt center to make a 48½" x 48½" quilt. Clip, swirl and press seams as necessary to achieve a flat seam.

5. Sew (2) 2½" x 48½" Fabric 2 strips to the top and bottom of the quilt. Press seams toward the Fabric 2 strips.

6. Sew (8) 6½" x 6½" Week Four: Thomas's Clock blocks together horizontally as shown to make a top/bottom border. Clip, swirl and press seams as necessary to achieve a flat seam. Make 2. Sew to the top and bottom of the quilt.

7. Sew (2) 2½" x 64½" Fabric 2 strips to the sides of the quilt to make a 52½" x 64½" quilt. Press seams toward the Fabric 2 strips.

8. Sew (8) 8½" x 8½" Week Five: Sous Chef Daisy blocks together vertically as shown to make a side border. Clip, swirl and press seams as necessary to achieve a flat seam. Make 2. Sew to the sides of the quilt. Press seams toward the Fabric 2 strips.

9. Sew (2) 2½" x 68½" Fabric 5 strips to the top and bottom of the quilt. Press seams toward the Fabric 5 strips.

10. Sew (2) 2½" x 68½" Fabric 5 strips to the sides of the quilt to make a 68½" x 68½" quilt. Press seams toward the Fabric 5 strips.

11. Sew (6) 12½" x 12½" Week Six: Plucky Rosamund blocks together horizontally as shown to make a top/bottom border. Clip, swirl and press seams as necessary to achieve a flat seam. Make 2. Sew to the top and bottom of the quilt.

Finishing

1. Piece the backing to measure 80" x 100" using a vertical seam.

2. Layer the quilt top, the batting and the backing. Quilt as desired.

3. Bind the quilt with double-fold binding made with the (9) 2½" x WOF Fabric 3 binding strips.

Finale One Quilt Assembly – Carson

Finale One Quilt Assembly - Cora

Finale One Quilt Assembly - Rose

Team Carson

Finale One Quilt

Team Rose

Team Cora

FOR THE BONUS BACKING PATTERN,
JUMP TO PAGE 103

Finale Two

Finished Quilt Size: 72" x 92"
Unfinished Quilt Size: 72½" x 92½"

Cutting

Color #	Team Cora	Team Carson	Team Rose	Cutting
2	A-7332-K1	A-7666-RK	A-7332-B1	Cut (6) 2½" x WOF strips. Piece strips end-to-end to make one long strip. From this, cut (2) 2½" x 48½" strips and (2) 2½" x 64½" strips.
3	A-7330-ET	A-7332-R	A-7616-EG	Cut (3) 2½" x WOF strips. From this, cut (2) 2½" x 20½" strips and (2) 2½" x 24½" strips. Cut (9) 2½" x WOF strips for binding.
5	A-7332-R	A-7332-N	A-7615-E	Cut (7) 2½" x WOF strips. Piece strips end-to-end to make one long strip. From this, cut (4) 2½" x 68½" strips.
Any	BACKING	BACKING	BACKING	5¾ yards
Any	BATTING	BATTING	BATTING	80" x 100"

Assembly (Refer to the Finale Two Quilt Assembly diagrams on pages 92, 93 and 94.)

1. Sew (2) 2½" x 20½" Fabric 3 strips to the top and bottom of the Week One: Manor House block. Press seams toward the Fabric 3 strips.

2. Sew (2) 2½" x 24½" Fabric 3 strips to the sides of the Week One: Manor House block to make a 24½" x 24½" quilt center. Press seams toward the Fabric 3 strips.

3. Sew (2) 12½" x 12½" Week Two: Earl's Pipe blocks together horizontally as shown to make a top/bottom border. Clip, swirl and press seams as necessary to achieve a flat seam. Make 2. Sew to the top and bottom of the quilt center.

4. Sew (4) 12½" x 12½" Week Three: Sarah's Daring blocks together vertically as shown to make a side border. Clip, swirl and press seams as necessary to achieve a flat seam. Make 2. Sew to the sides of the quilt enter to make a 48½" x 48½" quilt. Clip, swirl and press seams as necessary to achieve a flat seam.

5. Sew (2) 2½" x 48½" Fabric 2 strips to the top and bottom of the quilt. Press seams toward the Fabric 2 strips.

6. Sew (8) 6½" x 6½" Week Four: John's Loyalty blocks together horizontally as shown to make a top/bottom border. Clip, swirl and press seams as necessary to achieve a flat seam. Make 2. Sew to the top and bottom of the quilt.

7. Sew (2) 2½" x 64½" Fabric 2 strips to the sides of the quilt to make a 52½" x 64½" quilt. Press seams toward the Fabric 2 strips.

8. Sew (8) 8½" x 8½" Week Five: Master Chef Beryl blocks together vertically as shown to make a side border. Clip, swirl and press seams as necessary to achieve a flat seam. Make 2. Sew to the sides of the quilt. Press seams toward the Fabric 2 strips.

9. Sew (2) 2½" x 68½" Fabric 5 strips to the top and bottom of the quilt. Press seams toward the Fabric 5 strips.

10. Sew (2) 2½" x 68½" Fabric 5 strips to the sides of the quilt to make a 68½" x 68½" quilt. Press seams toward the Fabric 5 strips.

11. Sew (6) 12½" x 12½" Week Six: Energetic Rose blocks together horizontally as shown to make a top/bottom border. Clip, swirl and press seams as necessary to achieve a flat seam. Make 2. Sew to the top and bottom of the quilt.

Finishing

1. Piece the backing to measure 80" x 100" using a vertical seam.

2. Layer the quilt top, the batting and the backing. Quilt as desired.

3. Bind the quilt with double-fold binding made with the (9) 2½" x WOF Fabric 3 binding strips.

Finale Two Quilt Assembly - Carson

Finale Two Quilt Assembly - Cora

Finale Two Quilt Assembly - Rose

Finale Two Quilt

Team Carson

Team Rose

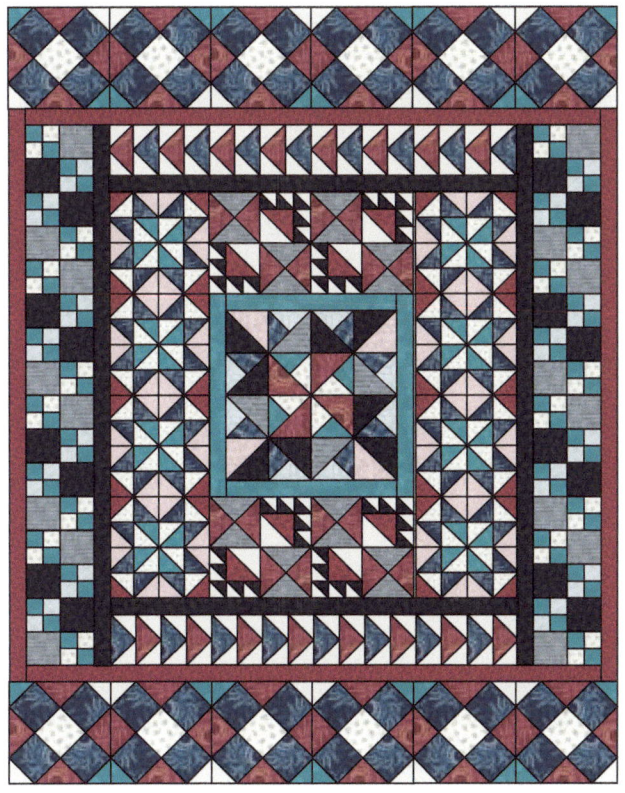

Team Cora

FOR THE BONUS BACKING PATTERN,
JUMP TO PAGE 103

Finale Three

Finished Quilt Size: 72" x 92"
Unfinished Quilt Size: 72½" x 92½"

Cutting

Color #	Team Cora	Team Carson	Team Rose	Cutting
2	A-7332-K1	A-7666-RK	A-7332-B1	Cut (6) 2½" x WOF strips. Piece strips end-to-end to make one long strip. From this, cut (2) 2½" x 48½" strips and (2) 2½" x 64½" strips.
3	A-7330-ET	A-7332-R	A-7616-EG	Cut (3) 2½" x WOF strips. From this, cut (2) 2½" x 20½" strips and (2) 2½" x 24½" strips. Cut (9) 2½" x WOF strips for binding.
5	A-7332-R	A-7332-N	A-7615-E	Cut (7) 2½" x WOF strips. Piece strips end-to-end to make one long strip. From this, cut (4) 2½" x 68½" strips.
Any	BACKING	BACKING	BACKING	5¾ yards
Any	BATTING	BATTING	BATTING	80" x 100"

Assembly (Refer to the Finale Three Quilt Assembly diagrams on pages 98, 99 and 100.)

1. Sew (2) 2½" x 20½" Fabric 3 strips to the top and bottom of the Week One: Manor House block. Press seams toward the Fabric 3 strips.

2. Sew (2) 2½" x 24½" Fabric 3 strips to the sides of the Week One: Manor House block to make a 24½" x 24½" quilt center. Press seams toward the Fabric 3 strips.

3. Sew (1) 12½" x 12½" Week Two: Lady's Tiara block to (1) 12½" x 12½" Week Two: Earl's Pipe block horizontally as shown to make a top/bottom border. Clip, swirl and press seams as necessary to achieve a flat seam. Make 2. Sew to the top and bottom of the quilt center.

4. Sew (4) 12½" x 12½" Week Three: Anna's Affection blocks together vertically as shown to make a left side border. Clip, swirl and press seams as necessary to achieve a flat seam. Sew to the left side of the quilt center. Clip, swirl and press seams as necessary to achieve a flat seam.

5. Sew (4) 12½" x 12½" Week Three: Sarah's Daring blocks together vertically as shown to make a right side border. Clip, swirl and press seams as necessary to achieve a flat seam. Sew to the right side of the quilt center to make a 48½" x 48½" quilt. Clip, swirl and press seams as necessary to achieve a flat seam.

6. Sew (2) 2½" x 48½" Fabric 2 strips to the top and bottom of the quilt. Press seams toward the Fabric 2 strips.

7. Sew (8) 6½" x 6½" Week Four: Thomas's Clock blocks together horizontally as shown to make a bottom border. Clip, swirl and press seams as necessary to achieve a flat seam. Sew to the bottom of the quilt. Press seams toward the Fabric 2 strips.

8. Sew (8) 6½" x 6½" Week Four: John's Loyalty blocks together horizontally as shown to make a top border. Clip, swirl and press seams as necessary to achieve a flat seam. Sew to the top of the quilt. Press seams toward the Fabric 2 strips.

9. Sew (2) 2½" x 64½" Fabric 2 strips to the sides of the quilt to make a 52½" x 64½" quilt. Press seams toward the Fabric 2 strips.

10. Sew (8) 8½" x 8½" Week Five: Sous Chef Daisy blocks together vertically as shown to make a left side border. Clip, swirl and press seams as necessary to achieve a flat seam. Sew to the left side of the quilt. Press seam toward the Fabric 2 strip.

11. Sew (8) 8½" x 8½" Week Five: Master Chef Beryl blocks together vertically as shown to make a right side border. Clip, swirl and press seams as necessary to achieve a flat seam. Sew to the right side of the quilt. Press seam toward the Fabric 2 strip.

12. Sew (2) 2½" x 68½" Fabric 5 strips to the top and bottom of the quilt. Press seams toward the Fabric 5 strips.

13. Sew (2) 2½" x 68½" Fabric 5 strips to the sides of the quilt to make a 68½" x 68½" quilt. Press seams toward the Fabric 5 strips.

14. Sew (6) 12½" x 12½" Week Six: Plucky Rosamund blocks together horizontally as shown to make a bottom border. Clip, swirl and press seams as necessary to achieve a flat seam. Sew to the bottom of the quilt. Press seams toward the Fabric 5 strips.

15. Sew (6) 12½" x 12½" Week Six: Energetic Rose blocks together horizontally as shown to make a top border. Clip, swirl and press seams as necessary to achieve a flat seam. Sew to the top of the quilt. Press seams toward the Fabric 5 strips.

Finishing

1. Piece the backing to measure 80" x 100" using a vertical seam.

2. Layer the quilt top, the batting and the backing. Quilt as desired.

3. Bind the quilt with double-fold binding made with the (9) 2½" x WOF Fabric 3 binding strips.

Finale Three Quilt Assembly - Carson

Finale Three Quilt Assembly – Cora

Finale Three Quilt Assembly – Rose

Team Carson

Finale Three Quilt

Team Rose

Team Cora

For the bonus backing pattern,
JUMP TO PAGE 103

Team Rose Quilt

by Cheri Little
FRISCO, TEXAS

Quilt along participants are free to play with the design, and there are literally hundreds of different combinations. We presented three options starting on page 83, but don't limit yourself to those options.

In this fine example of play, you can see Cheri did the Medley block sets each week, but in the end, decided to mix her sets together to create new and interesting designs within the quilt. Cheri had this to say about her experience, "Thank you for allowing me to share my quilt with you! I loved the mystery quilt along and look forward to the [next] one!"

Cheri's quilt is one of our favorite examples of the Quilt Your Own Story™ patterns, and you can see more of them in the Gallery starting on page 111 or on our website.

Cheri's playfulness didn't stop at her quilt top. Using a design inspired by the Egyptology backing, she created a fun quilt back using leftover fabrics from piecing her quilt top.

Egyptology
Week Eight

Egyptian Backing

The Egyptian Connection...

As you may know, George Herbert, the real 5th Earl of Carnarvon (whose estate, Highclere Castle, is the setting for Downton Abbey) was an amateur Egyptologist and financed the Howard Carter expedition to find and open King Tut's Tomb in 1922. Tutankhamun was an Egyptian pharaoh in the 18th dynasty during the period known as the New Kingdom.

Tutankhamun was nine years old when he ascended the throne, and died at age 19. He is known today as the "Boy King" and his popularity is due in part to the fact that his tomb was discovered nearly complete and undisturbed. There are some artifacts from his tomb at Highclere Castle; others travel around the world in museum exhibitions. King Tut's mummified remains are on display in a glass case inside his tomb.

Incorporating this backing into your quilt is a great way to connect the Egyptian history of Highclere to the Downton Abbey show, and give your quilt added color and shine.

The backing design is inspired by the Western wall of King Tut's tomb. One colorway is named for Tutankhamun himself, and the other for his wife, Ankhesenamun.

The backing provides enough fabric on all sides to have your quilt sent to a longarmer if desired. It is not necessary to center the quilt top to bottom, but centering side to side as closely as possible will preserve the look.

Tutankhamun

Ankhesenamun

Egyptology
Egyptian Backing

Unfinished Block Size: 82½" x 102½"

Yardage and Cutting

Color #	Tutankhamun	Ankhesenamun	Yardage	Yardage
11	 A-7624-LO	 A-7624-KO	3 yards	Cut (1) 33" x WOF strip. From strip, cut (1) 4½" x 33" strip. Cut in half lengthwise into (2) 4½" x 16½" rectangles. From remainder of strip, cut (4) 29" x 8½" rectangles. Cut (4) 3½" x WOF strips. Cut (1) 37" x WOF strip. From strip, cut (3) 7½" x 37" rectangles. Cut each strip in half lengthwise for (6) 7½" x 18½" rectangles. From remaining 37" length, cut (12) 2" x 30½" strips.
12	 A-7625-KT	 A-7621-MLT	1 yard	Cut (1) 6½" x WOF strip. From strip, cut (2) 6½" x 16½" rectangles. Cut (1) 4½" x WOF strip. From strip, cut (2) 4½" x 16½" rectangles. Cut (2) 5½" x WOF strips. Cut (3) 3½" x WOF strips.
13	 A-7619-MK	 A-7622-L	1⅞ yards	Cut (1) 16½" x WOF strip. From strip, cut (1) 16½" x 13½" rectangle. Cut (3) 3" x WOF strips. Cut (3) 3½" x WOF strips. Cut (12) 2½" x WOF strips.
14	 A-7622-KT	 A-7625-KT	2 yards	Cut (2) 8½" x WOF strips. From one strip, cut (1) 8½" x 25½" rectangle. From the remaining strip, cut (2) 8½" x 13" rectangles. Cut (6) 1¾" x WOF strips. Cut (3) 3½" x WOF strips. Cut (2) 6½" x WOF strips. Cut (2) 8½" x WOF strips.

Yardage and Cutting

Color #	Tutankhamun	Ankhesenamun	Yardage	Yardage
15	A-7620-MK	A-7620-MLN	¾ yard	Cut (4) 5½" x WOF strips.
16	A-7619-ML	A-7619-ML	¾ yard	Cut (3) 6½" x WOF strips.

Boat Ride Section (Make 1)

Finished Section Size: 24" x 82"
Unfinished Section Size: 24½" x 82½"

1. Sew (1) 4½" x 16½" Fabric 11 strip to (1) 4½" x 16½" Fabric 12 strip to make an 8½" x 16½" 11-12 rectangle. Press seam to the Fabric 11 strip. Make 2.

2. Sew (1) 8½" x 13" Fabric 14 rectangle to the right side of (1) 11-12 rectangle as shown to make an 8½" x 29" left center row. Press seam to Fabric 14 rectangle.

3. Sew the left center row between (2) 8½" x 29" Fabric 11 strips to make a 24½" x 29" Left Boat Ride unit. Press seams to the Fabric 11 strips.

4. Sew (1) 8½" x 13" Fabric 14 rectangle to the left side of (1) 11-12 rectangle as shown to make an 8½" x 29" right center row. Press seam to Fabric 14 rectangle.

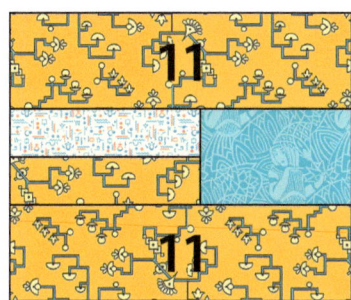

Left Boat Ride unit

5. Sew the right center row between (2) 8½" x 29" Fabric 11 strips to make a 24½" x 29" Right Boat Ride unit. Press seams to the Fabric 11 strips.

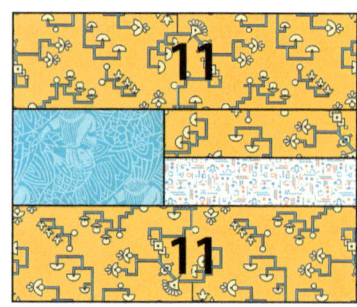

Right Boat Ride unit

6. Sew (1) 13½" x 16½" Fabric 13 rectangle between (2) 6½" x 16½" Fabric 12 strips to make a 12-13-12 rectangle. Press seams to Fabric 12 strips.

7. Sew (1) 8½" x 25½" Fabric 14 strip to the bottom of the 12-13-12 rectangle to make a 24½" x 25½" Center Boat Ride unit. Press seam to Fabric 14 strip.

8. Sew the Center Boat Ride unit between the Right Boat Ride unit and the Left Boat Ride unit as shown to complete a 24½" x 82½" Boat Ride section. Press seams open.

Center Boat Ride unit

Boat Ride section

Baboon Block *(Make 6)*

Finished Block Size: 15" x 15"
Unfinished Block Size: 15½" x 15½"

1. Sew (1) 5½" x WOF Fabric 12 strip between (2) 5½" x WOF Fabric 15 strips to make a three-strip panel. Press seams to Fabric 12 strip. Make 2 panels. Crosscut the (2) panels into 5½" segments for a total of (12) #1 segments measuring 5½" x 15½".

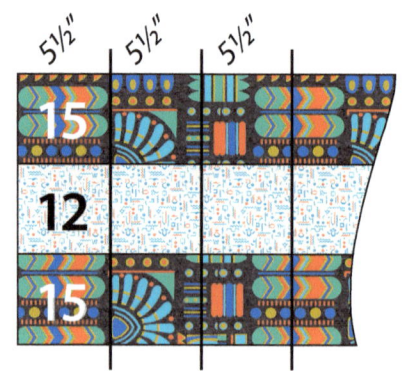

Cut 12

Cut 6

2. Sew (1) 3" x WOF Fabric 13 strip between (2) 1¾" x WOF Fabric 14 strips to make a three-strip panel. Press seams to Fabric 13 strip. Make 3 panels. Crosscut the (3) panels into 15½" segments for a total of (6) #2 segments measuring 15½" x 5½".

3. Sew (1) segment #2 between (2) of segment #1 as shown to make a 15½" x 15½" Baboon block. Press seams to segment #2. Make 6 blocks.

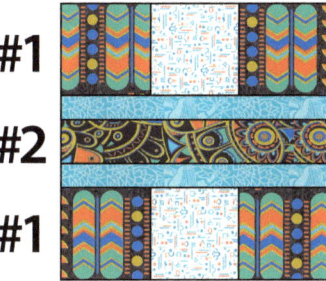

Hieroglyph Block (Make 6)

Finished Block Size: 15" x 15"
Unfinished Block Size: 15½" x 15½"

1. Sew (1) 3½" x WOF Fabric 13, (1) 3½" x WOF Fabric 14, (1) 3½" x WOF Fabric 12 and (1) 6½" x WOF Fabric 16 strip together in the given order as shown to make a four-strip panel. Press seams to Fabric 16 strip. Make 3 panels.

2. Crosscut the (3) panels into 15½" segments for a total of (6) 15½" x 15½" Hieroglyph blocks.

Cut 6

Divider (Make 3)

Finished Divider Size: 8" x 18"
Unfinished Divider Size: 8½" x 18½"

1. Sew (1) 2½" x WOF Fabric 13 strip between (2) 3½" x WOF Fabric 11 strips to make a three-strip panel. Press seams to Fabric 11 strip. Make 2 panels.

2. Crosscut the (2) panels into 18½" segments for a total of (3) 8½" x 18½" Dividers.

Cut 3

Baboon/Hieroglyph Sections A & B

Finished Section Size: 18" x 82"
Unfinished Section Size: 18½" x 82½"

1. Sew (1) Baboon block to (1) Hieroglyph block as shown to make a two-block unit.

2. Sew a 2" x 30½" Fabric 11 strip to the top and bottom of the unit to make an 18½" x 30½" two-block panel #1. Make 3 of panel #1.

Panel #1

Panel #2

3. Sew (1) Baboon block to (1) Hieroglyph block as shown to make a two-block unit.

4. Sew a 2" x 30½" Fabric 11 strip to the top and bottom of the unit to make an 18½" x 30½" two-block panel #2. Make 3 of panel #2.

5. Lay out (2) 7½" x 18½" Fabric 11 rectangles, (1) Panel #1, (1) Panel #2 and (1) Divider as shown to make an 18½" x 82½" Baboon/Hieroglyph section A. Make 2.

Panel #1 *Divider* *Panel #2*

6. Lay out (2) 7½" x 18½" Fabric 11 rectangles, (1) Panel #1, (1) Panel #2 and (1) Divider as shown to make an 18½" x 82½" Baboon/Hieroglyph section B.

Panel #2 *Divider* *Panel #1*

Assembly

Finished Backing Size: 82" x 102"
Unfinished Backing Size: 82½" x 102½"

1. Sew the short ends of (2) 6½" x WOF Fabric 14 strips together to make a long strip. Press seams open. Crosscut the long strip into (1) 6½" x 82½" length.

2. Sew the short ends of (2) 8½" x WOF Fabric 14 strips together to make a long strip. Press seams open. Crosscut the long strip into (1) 8½" x 82½" length.

3. Sew the short ends of (10) 2½" x WOF Fabric 13 strips together to make a long strip. Press seams open. Crosscut the long strip into (5) 2½" x 82½" lengths.

4. Lay out the assorted 82½" strips, the Boat Ride section, the (3) Baboon/Hieroglyph sections and the (3) Dividers as shown.

5. Sew the strips and sections together vertically to complete an 82½" x 102½" backing. Clip and press seams as necessary to achieve a flat seam.

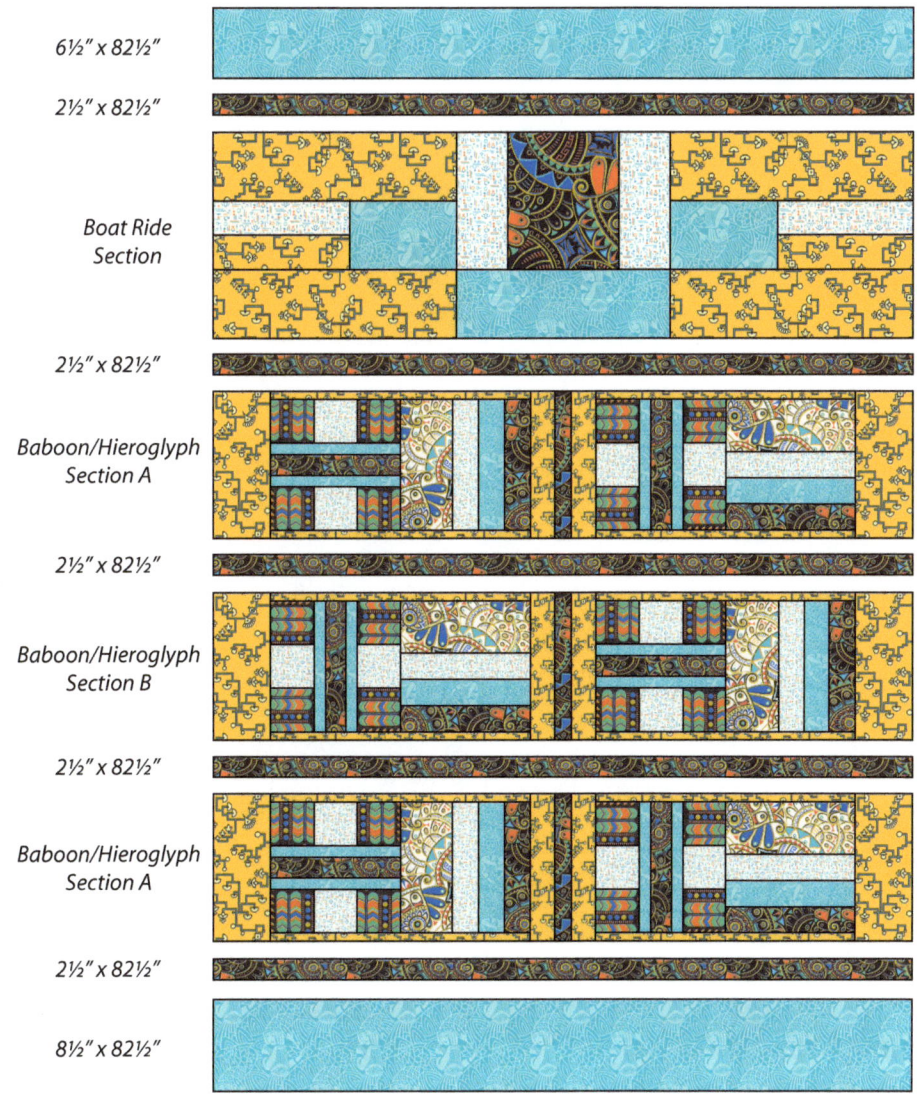

Tutankhamun

Ankhesenamun

Quilter's Gallery

Quilter's Gallery

Strolling Down Downton Abbey
by Judy Taylor   BELLINGHAM, WA

To get the size she wanted, Judy didn't use all the blocks in the top. Instead she rearranged and added some narrow borders. She used the remaining blocks as part of the backing along with leftover fabric.

Cora's Mystery Quilt
by Marjorie Campany   PALM COAST, FL

We think Her Ladyship would approve of the neat job Marjorie did with this quilt. Destined to become a family heirloom!

Richy's Team Carson
by Richy Lainson   PARSHALL, ND

Proving that the French and English can get along, Richy added a continental twist to the Team Carson quilt by using French General fabrics.

English Manor Mystery Quilt
by Leslie Sams   EFFINGHAM, IL

The weather would probably do it in, but we think Leslie's quilt looks great with her house (And her extra borders are outstanding!)

When Bali Meets Downton
by Rita Bigelow   ANKENY, IA

Done in warm gold and purple batiks, "These were toasty fabrics to work with during a cold Midwest winter! Thanks again, Ebony, for a fun adventure to share with friends known and as yet unmet."

Jana's Cora Quilt
by Jana Daniel   BROWNFIELD, TX

Jana mixed up the blocks and added some strips and squares of leftover fabric as borders for her Cora quilt.

Cherry's Egyptian Backing
by Cherry Jones   HATTIESBURG, MS

Sometimes you make a quilt just like the picture; sometimes you tell your own story. Cherry started with the Egyptian pattern and had fun with it!

Mandy's Rose Quilt
by Mandy McBeth Dowdy
GREENWOOD SPRINGS, MS

Mandy took some liberty with the quilt assembly, varying the strips between rows, for instance. Because the program had so much flexibility, she felt good about doing it.

Quilter's Gallery

Carson in Retirement
by Linda Holzhueter   WATERLOO, WI

Linda went all in with the mystery quilt for the front, the Egyptian pattern for the back and even a half-size! She retired just before starting, and bravely permitted her husband to pick the fabrics for the mini.

Jean's English Mystery
by Jean Smith   WILLIAMSBURG, VA

Team Rose for the win! This nicely executed quilt in the Rose colors makes for a cozy and lovely bedroom.

Mary Ann's English Manor
by Mary Ann Evans   MILLERSVIEW, TX

What's black & white & red all over? Mary Ann's English Manor quilt! She followed the medley using her own selection of black, white, gray and red fabrics.

Love's Knot
by Donna Marie Savoy   MIRAMICHI, NB, CANADA

By following the block patterns but using a mix of florals and solids, Donna has created a unique quilt, full of life and color.

Marsha's English Manor
by Marsha Day   ANDALUSIA, AL

Marsha used some Downton Abbey fabrics and mixed in some others for her own striking take on the English Manor Team Cora quilt.

Pamela's English Manor
by Pamela Jackson   PUYALLUP, WA

Pamela used this year's pattern and the previous year's Lady Mary fabrics to put her own spin on "this wonderfully designed quilt." She also added extra blocks and borders.

English Manor Mirabelle
by Christina Teague   FOLSOM, LA

Using fabrics from Fig Tree & Co.'s Mirabelle line, Christina made the top and bottom rows go edge to edge and added an additional border of flying geese to lower the drape on the sides.

English Manor/Cora Quilt
by Teresa Lahtinen Smith   VIRGINIA, MN

Teresa quilted with Team Cora, but forged her own path with her block placement and interesting borders.

Quilter's Gallery

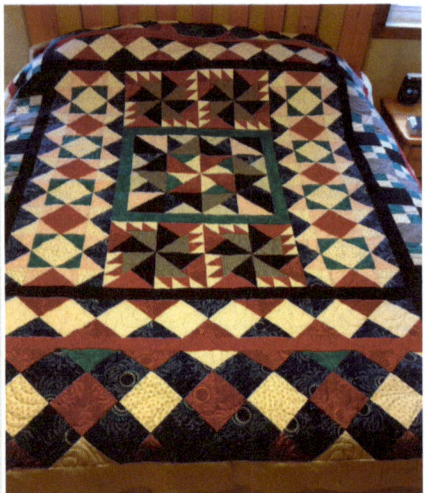

Sherry's Team Cora
by Sherry Meyer   DELIA, AB, CANADA

Sherry quilted with Team Cora. Her neat and symmetrical quilt beautifully reflects the care and character of Cora.

Leslie's English Manor
by Leslie Pernas-Giz   MELBOURNE, FL

Leslie joined the big leagues with her first "serious" quilt. She loved the variations but followed the pattern as presented. She especially enjoyed seeing the King Tut backing and decided to use it.

Abbey Rose
by Trudy Teshima   ORANGE, CA

Trudy quilted with Team Rose, but in her own way. "This is Rose, from my own fabrics. She's always lovely in pink and needed a garden of green surrounded by the sky of blue."

English Manor in Batiks
by Janeen Pearson   ALTOONA, IA

Janeen busted her own stash of batiks for this quilt using the medley patterns, and had Jessie Ziegler of Threaded Quilting Studio do the machine quilting.

Nancy S's English Manor
by Nancy Austin Swanwick   FORT SCOTT, KS

Nancy quilted a Team Carson-like top with the medley patterns and a few fabric substitutions to make it her own. She also made half-scale and quarter-scale versions.

Sheri's Rose
by Sheri Salatin   SWOOPE, VA

Not quite a Rose colorway, but certainly lively. Sheri's quilt shows how you can start with a pattern but tell your own story with your quilts.

Angela's English Manor
by Angela Oldridge   DIDSBURY, AB, CANADA

Angela's unique placement of blocks in her Carson quilt makes for some very interesting geometric patterns.

Quilter's Gallery

Nancy G's Team Rose
by Nancy Gillooly   AUBURN, NY

Nancy made the blocks each week in the Rose colorway, but put them together in a totally different setting to make this unique quilt.

Mary Jane W's Team Cora
by Mary Jane Weddle   CAMPBELLSVILLE, KY

Mary loved this project. "Thanks, Ebony, for this fun activity!!" she said. She quilted with Team Cora and chose to use the Egyptian fabrics with the King Tut backing.

Mary Jane T's English Manor
by Mary Jane Tingle   MOUNTAIN BROOK, AL

Showing no preference for upstairs or downstairs, Mary Jane mixed Earl's Pipe with Anna, John, Daisy and Rosamund in her Cora colorway quilt.

Sharon's Carson Quilt
by Sharon Moorehead   OLYMPIA, WA

Sharon's quilt is classic Carson: everything is neat, in order, and done with excellence.

A Spot of Cream in Your Tea
by Linda Walters   CHINO HILLS, CA

Going off in a completely different color direction, Linda chose fabrics from "Little Black Dress" by Moda for her quilt. "A Spot of Cream in Your Tea" is certainly refreshing!

Wanda's English Manor
by Wanda Stephens   BIG SPRING, TX

In a representation of old meets older, Wanda crossed eras (and continents!) by using Civil War reproduction fabrics in her English Manor quilt.

Nyla's Team Cora
by Nyla Poser   BUCKLEY, WA

In another French/English pairing, Nyla chose some Downton Abbey fabrics and some French General fabrics for her take on the Team Cora quilt.

Wildflower Downton Abbey Mystery Quilt
by Wendi Weston   SACRAMENTO, CA

Appropriately for making a Team Rose quilt, Wendi used florals from her personal stash and had a great time learning new skills.

Solid as a Rock

By Ebony Love
GRAYSLAKE IL

Ebony always wonders what a quilt will look like all made in solids, and this one she loved well enough to dip into her cache of Robert Kaufman Kona to piece a quilt of her own.

Color #	Swatch	Robert Kaufman Kona
	Ebony's Solids	
1		1225 Medium Pink
2		0359 Pepper
3		1183 Jade Green
4		1336 Slate
5		1551 Rich Red
6		1028 Blue
7		0140 Nightfall
8		1087 Coral
9		1323 Sand
10		1339 Snow

Like to make your own solids version?

Follow the quilt instructions for any of the color ways listed in the book, substituting the fabrics listed here. This quilt most closely resembles the Team Cora color way, so please refer to those block diagrams for fabric placement.

Have fun!

EDeN™ System Chart

EDeN™ Number (finished size)	Rotary (cut size)	Sizzix®	AccuQuilt GO!®	AccuQuilt Studio™
HST-2	Cut a 2-7/8" square; cut in half along one diagonal (makes 2)	656685, 657611, 659831—Sizzix Die—Half-Square Triangles, 2 1/2" Finished Square	55018, 55021—Value Die (2 1/2" Triangles) OR 55063—GO! Half Square—2" Finished Triangle Multiples	50161, 50272—Studio Half Square—2" Finished Triangle
HST-3	Cut a 3-7/8" square; cut in half along one diagonal (makes 2)	656686, 657612—Sizzix Die—Half-Square Triangles, 3 1/2" Finished Square	55009—GO! Half Square—3" Finished Triangle OR 55048—GO! Bountiful Baskets (3 1/2" cut)	50163, 50278—Studio Half Square—3" Finished Triangle
HST-4	Cut a 4-7/8" square; cut in half along one diagonal (makes 2)	656677, 657613, 657832—Sizzix Die—Half-Square Triangles, 4 1/2" Finished Square	55031—GO! Half Square—4" Finished Triangle	50000—Studio Square—4 7/8" (cut in half on the diagonal) OR 50005, 50270—Studio Half Square—4" Finished Triangle
HST-5	Cut a 5-7/8" square; cut in half along one diagonal (makes 2)	657637—Sizzix Die—Half-Square Triangles, 5 1/2" Finished Square	NONE	50273—Studio Half Square—5" Finished Triangle
QST-4	Cut a 5-1/4" square; cut in half along both diagonals (makes 4)	657614—Sizzix Originals Die—Triangle, 2 5/8"H x 4 1/2"W Unfinished OR 657166, 659852—Sizzix Die—Triangles, 2 1/2"H x 4 1/2"W Unfinished	55047, 55316—GO! Quarter Square 4" Finished Triangles	50271—Studio Quarter Square—4" Finished Triangle
QST-5	Cut a 6-1/4" square; cut in half along both diagonals (makes 4)	657620—Sizzix Bigz L Die—Triangle, 3 1/8"H x 5 1/2"W Unfinished	NONE	50274—Studio Quarter Square—5" Finished Triangle
QST-6	Cut a 7-1/4" square; cut in half along both diagonals (makes 4)	657621—Sizzix Clear Die—Triangle, 3 5/8"H x 6 1/2"W Unfinished OR 657171—Sizzix Die—Triangles, 3 1/2"H x 6 1/2"W Unfinished	55002—GO! Triangle 4 7/8"	50034, 50277—Studio Quarter Square—6" Finished Triangle

© LoveBug Studios, 2011-2015. You may freely copy these charts for personal use only. Full versions available on http://equivalentdienotation.com

EDeN™ System Chart

EDeN™ Number (finished size)	Rotary (cut size)	Sizzix®	AccuQuilt GO!®	AccuQuilt Studio™
SOP-6	Cut a strip 4-3/4" wide; subcut to 4-3/4"	NONE	55019—GO! Square—4 3/4"	50035, 50144—Studio Square on Point—4 3/4"
SQ-2	Cut a strip 2-1/2" wide; subcut to 2-1/2"	656674, 656682, 657607—Sizzix Die—Squares, 2" Finished OR STR-2	55059—GO! Square 2 1/2" Multiples OR 55018, 55021 – Value Die (2 1/2" Square) OR STR-2	50124, 50204, 50603—Studio Square—2 1/2" OR STR-2
SQ-4	Cut a strip 4-1/2" wide; subcut to 4-1/2"	657609—Sizzix Bigz Die—Square, 4" Finished OR STR-4	55018, 55021—Value Die (4 1/2" Square) OR 55060—GO! Square—4 1/2" Multiples OR STR-4	50015, 50123 – Studio Square—4 1/2" OR STR-4
STR-2	Cut a LOF strip X 2-1/2" wide	656681, 656688, 658328, 658330—Sizzix Die—Strips, 2 1/2" Wide use the lengthwise grain for borders	55014, 55017—GO! Strip Cutter 2 1/2" use the lengthwise grain for borders	50056, 50612—Studio Strip Cutter 2 1/2" use the lengthwise grain for borders

© LoveBug Studios, 2011-2015. You may freely copy these charts for personal use only. Full versions available on http://equivalentdienotation.com

A Few Notes

- All block sizes are stated in finished block measurements, assuming a ¼" seam allowance unless otherwise indicated.

- Blocks will be charted in as many sizes as possible using dies for all units, up to 24", as space permits.

- Sometimes, it is necessary to substitute a die shape that is a bit larger than needed in order to make a block which finishes at the specified size.

  These dies will be included if the unit can be easily squared-up to the correct size after piecing. These will be noted in the block charts.

- When a strip cutter is specified by itself for a unit that is square, you are meant to use the strip cutter to cut strips, then rotate the strips 90° on the same die and re-cut the fabric to make squares.

- When a strip cutter is specified to cut diamonds, you are meant to cut strips first, then rotate the strip the indicated number of degrees to cut diamonds. This will be easier if you mark your dies in advance.

- When a strip cutter is shown in combination with another die (e.g., 2" strip cutter AND 3½" strip cutter), this is an indication to cut strips on one die, then rotate 90° and layer on the second die to cut rectangles.

- Fabric yardage is assumed to be 40" wide and rounded up to the nearest ¼ yard, and is calculated ONLY for the original block given. Please note that the quilt layouts provided have not been personally tested; you are encouraged to perform your own fabric calculations if you need to be more accurate.

- **WOF** = width of fabric; **LOF** = length of fabric; **RSU** = right side up; **WSU** = wrong side up; **RST** = right sides together.

www.ingramcontent.com/pod-product-compliance
Lightning Source LLC
Chambersburg PA
CBHW042029150426
43199CB00002B/9